'A thoroughly engaging series of essays to open up discussion on the construction of masculinity, male desire, male defences against intimacy and so on, which will be of interest to both men and women. As the varied contributions illuminate the conscious and unconscious attitudes and structures that inform masculinity, they provide us with a new stimulus for the desperately needed dialogue on sexual politics and gender relations.'

Susie Orbach

Peter Bradbury is a writer living in London and working with a radical art collective, Paddington Printshop. He has published poetry and criticism in North America and Australia, and his recent work on male sexuality has appeared in *Achilles Heel* and *Radical America*.

Richard Dyer studied at St Andrew's University and Birmingham University; apart from a brief period in the theatre, he has worked chiefly in adult and higher education. He was a member of the Gay Liberation Front and Gay Left, and is a counsellor with the gay counselling agency, Friend. He has written for *Screen* and *Jump Cut*; his previous books include *Gays and Film* (BFI), *Stars* (BFI) and *Heavenly Bodies* (Macmillan). He now lectures at Warwick University.

Tony Eardley lives in London and has been involved in sexual politics since the early 1970s. He studied classics and English literature at Oxford University, and Social Administration at Bristol. He was a member of the editorial collective of *Achilles Heel* and has contributed articles to that and other periodicals. He has been active in local community politics – housing, under fives day care – and is currently employed as an advice worker for the National Council for One Parent Families.

Jeff Hearn lives in Bradford, where he is a lecturer at the University. For the last six years he has been involved in men's groups and child care campaigning, and more recently in a local men's anti-sexist newsletter collective. He has published widely on social and political issues, including patriarchy, public sector cuts and men at work; last year he produced a short book *Birth and Afterbirth: a Materialist Account* (Achilles Heel) on men's relationship to birth and children.

Martin Humphries is a poet and writer who lives in London. His publications include *Mirrors* and *Searching for a Destination*. He has been involved with gay politics since the late 1970s and was a member of the editorial collective of *Achilles Heel* until 1984. Currently he works part-time with his lover, who runs a cinema archive, and with Gay Sweatshop. As well as writing, he worked in theatre, film and video; his work includes a one-man audio visual show based on his poetry.

Andy Metcalf studied medicine and planning, worked in a number of industries for a while and wrote, with Andrew Friend, *Slump City – The Politics of Mass Unemployment* (Pluto Press). He likes playing tennis and writing poetry. He was in a men's group for a number of years. At present, he works in film and has just completed a film about the history of the nuclear energy project. His previous work in film includes the series 'About Men' and the comedy *Domestic Bliss*. He has two children and lives in London.

Andy Moye has worked as a town planner, part-time polytechnic lecturer, housing adviser for single people, and researcher. He is currently employed as a community worker in north London. He is a former member of the editorial collective of *Achilles Heel*.

Thomas J. Ryan is an American psychotherapist who has been living and working in England for the past sixteen years. In addition to his research interest in sexuality, he divides his time between his psychotherapy practice and work with the Arbours Association. He lives with his family in north London.

Vic Seidler teaches social theory and philosophy at Goldsmith's College, University of London. He has been involved with *Achilles Heel* since its inception and was part of the group that edited *One Dimensional Marxism* (Allison and Busby). He lives with Anna and their son Daniel in Dalston, East London, and is currently writing a book on liberal moral theory to be published by Routledge & Kegan Paul.

The Sexuality of Men

Edited by Andy Metcalf and
Martin Humphries

Pluto  Press

London and Sydney

First published in 1985 by Pluto Press Limited,
The Works, 105a Torriano Avenue, London NW5 2RX
and Pluto Press Australia Limited, PO Box 199, Leichhardt,
New South Wales 2040, Australia

7   6   5   4   3   2

89   88   87   86   85

Phototypeset by *Sunrise Setting,* Torquay, Devon

Printed in Great Britain by Guernsey Press, Guernsey, CI.

British Library Cataloguing in Publication Data

The Sexuality of men.
  1. Men—Sexual behavior
  I. Metcalf, Andy   II. Humphries, Martin
  612′.6′088041   HQ28

  ISBN 0-86104-638-2

Contents

Acknowledgements

This book has, in many ways, grown out of our experience of working in *Achilles Heel*. We'd like to thank all those who worked with us on the magazine. In addition, Martin Humphries would like to thank Noël Greig and Tom Swan – the men he shares communal living with – and those at Crystal for their support. And Ronald Grant for his love and because he was always there when needed. Andy Metcalf sends his thanks to Paul Atkinson, Paul Morrison, Andy Moye and Susie Orbach for their help and friendship. And to Gillian Slovo for her support and love. Finally we'd like to thank the contributors for their work and perseverance, and Paul Crane of Pluto for his editorial help.

Andy Metcalf and Martin Humphries

1. Introduction

This is a book about male sexuality – about what it means to a man to know another person intimately. It is about the feelings, the absences, and the fears that men bring to their sexual relationships. It would be nice to have put a more joyful phrase in that list, but these days sex is a fraught affair for many men. It is a topic we break away from or parry with a joke. There is a silence about it; in all the voluminous literature on sex and sexuality, there is very little on male sexuality as such. Most of the men contributing to this book have discovered that it is also a hidden subject, resistant to their first investigations. It seems as if it's so much an accepted part of everyday life that it is invisible.

And yet this is strange when you consider that we are bombarded with extreme images of the sexual male, from Clint Eastwood with his oversized gun, to an endless stream of male rock vocalists clutching their microphones, to the posturings of military men. Every year these representations become harder, more violent and assertive. Popular versions of what it is to be a 'real man' have become so outlandish as to prompt the idea that all is not as it should be for the male sex. This book explores this idea and develops the findings of Shere Hite's book on male sexuality:[1] that beneath the macho posing and the bedroom performance, many men have unsure and conflicting feelings about their sexuality.

From an entirely different direction, feminism has put male sexuality on the political agenda. Feminist campaigns have made visible everyday violence against women, male domination at work and in the home, and the exploits of the pornography industry. The women's movement, whilst campaigning about the consequences of male sexuality have not seen it as their business to understand or explore the nature and motivations of male sexual behaviour. The problem of men has been established; but why they are such a problem has not received much attention. And yet the ways of thinking which inform this book have only been able to surface because of the pioneering work of feminist discussion and scholarship. As feminism has become a major social and political force many men have succumbed to the temptation of taking evasive action. They have kept their heads down, pretended to be good boys – or if politically inclined, have argued that these issues are quite secondary to the struggle for socialism.

In gay politics male sexuality has been on the agenda since the early seventies. One of the early demands of gay liberation was for heterosexual men to 'come out' – which meant, at that time, that men should recognize that their sexuality is not necessarily fixed in one mould. Since then, questioning and debating masculinity and male sexuality has been an integral part of the gay movement. The patterns of gay men's sexual expression may be different from heterosexual men's – gay men may have more sex, with more partners in more varied ways – but the absences and fears persist. There has been a growing recognition that gay sexuality has to be seen not as a completely distinct form of sexuality, but as a part of male sexuality as a whole, illuminating it from its particular viewpoint. The gay perspective has a way of seeing through the rhetoric of masculinity and exposing the hollowness of the image. In part this is because such a perspective focuses on men desiring men and by doing so throws into relief the ways heterosexual men back away from the panoply of meanings surrounding the sexual domain. Men want sex, have sex, but don't allow themselves to be the object of sexual desire. Women, and not men, should be the bearers of the sexual. They should be the ones to be desired. They should contain within their 'being', their social relations, their sense of fashion, all the promises of sex. Gay men blow that careful distinction.

Traditionally men have been quite at ease spouting off on any subject under the sun except one: themselves. But gradually men have, over the last decade, begun to address that subject. Individually, in groups, through training or therapy, we have begun to ask the simple questions of who we are, and why we act as we do. Mind you, we have often asked these questions in highly convoluted and circuitous ways, as this account by the women tutors of a course on 'Sexual Politics for Men' makes clear:

> Talking personally proved in some cases to be extremely difficult – years of speaking in the third person and conceptualizing at a macro-political level meant that a request to discuss the experience, for instance, of learning not to cry, might provoke a quite impersonal discourse on the process of socialization . . . We felt that if men do not allow space for, or listen to women properly, neither do they offer openings to each other, and especially not for the expression of feelings. One of the most interesting discussions for us as women was a confirmation of what we had experienced as a major problem about men: their inability to express warmth. We wanted them to confront this for themselves. To do this, we asked them to tell other people in their group what it was they liked about them. In one group, this was met first with silence, then with ten minutes assorted displacement activity, then with an attack on us for setting such an absurd question – after all they didn't really know each other. It took twenty five minutes before one man turned to another and said: 'I like you'.[2]

It has proved a hard and lengthy business for us to become able to express how we feel directly and openly. Much of the writing and discussion about masculinity over the last decade has focused on this, either directly or implicitly, through the adoption of a confessional stance. It has even become a cliché to state that many men have trouble communicating emotionally, and this has provoked superior and bored comments from academic and journalistic arbiters of fashion in sexual politics. And yet the implications of this understanding are of great significance. If the vast majority of men are emotionally illiterate then the social construction of gender, of masculinity, creates an absence, a loss, a silence at the heart of men's social relations. Both Tom Ryan's and Vic Seidler's pieces show that the very creation of masculinity, within a gender-divided society, during infancy, necessarily involves this silence. Much of this book is concerned with exploring the consequences of modern man's lack of emotional knowledge and language. And those consequences are hardly trivial: sexual violence towards women, the allure of pornography, the difficulties we experience in maintaining intimacy with our wives and lovers.

Reserved, strung out, trying on Jack Nicholson tricks, we approach sex like teenagers. It's the magic fix; it's a slice of the natural; it's our only entry back into the subjective. This is a heavy load to bring to an activity that is supposed to be natural and spontaneous. But whether or not we feel spontaneous, it is clear that sex for both men and women carries many more meanings than an erotic impulse. Through skin to skin contact, stroking and caressing, it mimics early infant life and can reinvoke powerful levels of well-being. In its symbolic recreation of our infant existence, sexual activity may become the vehicle for a number of conflicting emotions: love, hostility or dependency. It comes in a whole context of learned and assumed attitudes, from playground boasts to the instructions in a sex manual.

Sex may be 'natural' – but all that says is that the 'natural' is neither simple nor indivisible. For men, sexual activity carries additional loads – it is the one area of our life in which we feel able to express our feelings, to let slip some of the masks of masculinity, to become vulnerable for a short time. Sex for men seems less of a pure animal act, despite our fantasies, and more of a bulky portmanteau we stagger around with, desperate to unlock, but with rusted keys. Here, mingled with desire, there's the need for tenderness, the need to talk, to let skin speak to skin; there's misery that only sex seems able to right. It serves as a rush at bridging the gender divide; an attempt to bring a junior partner into line; a method of resolving feelings of unconnectedness to oneself and to others. A whole bundle of emotions, which seem to have little to do with the erotic. The hold sex has over men arises from the fact that sex is linked with motives and forces other than the need for sexual satisfaction.

Here perhaps we have clues as to the underlying causes of the male model of sexuality: driven not liberated, organized around orgasm, permeated with anxieties about performance and achievement. There are many strands to such a compulsive sexuality. At school enormous status is conferred on boys who 'make it' with girls – or who can convincingly boast of a conquest. Sex itself is given almost mystic powers – as one fifth former points out: 'You think that when you have sex you're going to walk into a bedroom a boy and come out a man, deep voice, big chest sticking out and muscles all over you. And you can go round and spit the world in the eye.'[3] That also means it is a prized possession for which all sorts of lies and tricks are legitimate. In such a way we become alienated from our desires and sexual feelings. In sex education classes – at school and in our culture generally – sex is portrayed as an act, a set of mechanical aims and skills without any emotional content. While girls will endlessly discuss the ramifications of the romances they are involved in, stretching and developing their understanding of emotions, boys don't talk much about this, keeping their friends at bay and rarely discussing problems in their love life with their male friends. It is a pattern that often persists through adult life.

The proliferation of sex manuals has emphasized anxiety about performance, constantly playing on the theme of success and failure – bigger and better orgasms or sexual boredom. The truly sexual male is portrayed as being able to deploy a wide and varied repertoire of skills and expertise in order to satisfy a woman. In terms of women's sexual pleasure, such an education has obviously been an advance on the traditional 'wham bam thank you ma'am' practice. But the problem with sexology is that while it has both exacerbated and keyed into the anxieties of modern masculinity, it has skated over the conflicts men experience about their sexual practice. These books never contain a word about male fears of women's sexuality. Men's own sexual needs are taken for granted – to get more of 'it' and better quality 'it'. That men may have needs that don't fit the compulsive model is rarely acknowledged. The nearest sex manuals come to a critique of male compulsions is to stress that lots of foreplay is a good thing and the way to be a good lover. Heaven forbid the notion that we might actually question whether we want all of this sex we are urged to consume. The most pernicious aspect of all this is that men, dodging behind the banner of women's sexual pleasure, have allowed their own complex and emotional needs to be unacknowledged and even to remain unknown to themselves. They are left to lie underneath the surface of the smoothed out moves, jarring them occasionally, flaring up in surly and resentful episodes, or exploding in violent anger. A dialogue, establishing and developing the emotional contexts and needs which both women and men bring to their sex lives, has been conspicuous in its absence. Little chance of a dialogue when men have been so silent, have channelled all their needs into the act of 'love-making'.

The key to understanding the quality of much male sexuality seems to lie in the link between sex and gender identity. Gender identity is that sense at the core of one's self of being either female or male. It has been strongly argued that sexuality is a crucial factor in the maintenance of masculine gender identity, but not necessarily that of female gender identity. Ethel Person writes of this:

> There is a wealth of evidence to suggest that in this culture, genital sexual activity is a prominent feature in the maintenance of masculine gender, while it is a variable feature in feminine gender. Thus an impotent man always feels that his masculinity, and not just his sexuality, is

threatened. In men gender appears to lean on sexuality. It is impossible to locate a physically intact man who has never achieved orgasm by any route whatsoever who does not have significant psychopathology. In males the need for sexual performance is so great that performance anxiety is the leading cause of secondary impotence. The vast array of male 'perversions' (in both type and number) in contrast to women, may be testimony to the male need to preserve sexuality against long odds . . . In women, gender identity and self-worth can be consolidated by other means . . . while women may suffer the consequences of sexual inhibition, sexual expression is not critical to personality development. Many women have the capacity to abstain from sex without negative psychological consequences (the problem for women is that they are often denied the legal right of sexual refusal).[4]

The argument then is that male sexuality so often has a driven quality because it is through genital sex that a relatively fragile male identity can be consolidated. It is interesting in this context that in the Hite report on male sexuality, one of the reasons male respondents most often gave for wanting sex was the sense of affirmation or self-validation gained through sex. A recent feminist account suggests that masculinity is constructed as a defence against original anger with mothers. As such, much of male sexuality can be understood as shoring up a shaky sense of maleness.[5] From this perspective, the creation of gender identity in the first years of life is the crucial stage in the formation of male sexuality. The subsequent learning of male roles, the playground bragging, the reliance on porn, all feed upon, and attempt to consolidate, the fragile structure laid down in infancy. The silence of men is a little more understandable in the light of these ideas.

Tom Ryan, in chapter 2, explores the fragility of male gender identity within the context of the contemporary sexual division of labour. In this he is extending a debate live in both psychoanalysis and feminism.[6] His discussion is based upon an understanding of the consequences of the primacy of the mother in infant rearing and the relative absence of the father, in this society. This is important for a number of reasons: it is a step in the creation of a psycholanalytic perspective on male sexuality which embraces, rather than denies – as does so much modern psychoanalytic theory – the social and historical. Such a perspective underpins a seachange now occurring in men's relationships to their children. Partly as a result of unemployment, many men are coming to realize the preciousness of these relationships; many are determined to be fully involved in the birth of their children, others are getting involved in political activities around these issues – fighting for increased paternity leave, flexible working hours, job sharing, and an expanded nursery sector. In my own union, this year's annual conference saw more resolutions on paternity leave than on any other subject.[7] For men to have strong loving relationships with their children is not only an essential step in securing more egalitarian relationships between women and men, it is also a powerful way of transforming the sensibilities and sexualities of both sons and fathers.[8]

Two broad themes run through this book. One is that much of male sexuality can be understood only if the family constellation around the infant is brought into the picture, and psychoanalytic approaches discussed. The other theme concerns the changes which have occurred over the last thirty years in women's place in the world. It is difficult to grasp the real meaning of change. It is a concept which has been degraded through its use in Sunday supplements; and denied validity by the high priests of post-structuralist thought. Despite this, it seems necessary to pause and consider the changes which have rattled the windows and blown the roofs off a good many family homes over the last quarter of a century.

While we were researching the film series 'About Men'[9] in the Midlands we talked to a number of men who gave their wives a fixed amount from their pay packet for the housekeeping. They did not disclose to their wives how much they were paid and avoided joint financial discussions. The majority of men we interviewed no longer exercised this sort of control, but we were taken aback by the number who did. Our surprise came from stumbling across a window into the past: a rigid hierarchy undisturbed by the women's movement, where women stayed at home and lived within the parameters set by men – for there seemed to be precious few escape routes. Even though it was never like that for everyone, it is still an image to set against today: when under conditions of prolonged recession over 40 per cent of the paid workforce are women; when the core of the working class movement – male manual workers in heavy industry – have been decimated by closure and redundancy; when women can control their own fertility with far greater safety than before. These are very basic changes – and they have enabled a growing number of women to lead lives independently of men. The scale of this is by no means marginal: seven out of ten divorces are initiated by women; in the inner city areas of large cities, around a third of all households are now single parent families headed by women. The representation of the family in the media as headed by a man, in work, with children, and an economically dependent wife, only applies to a very small fraction of households in this country. The TV images just don't measure up to the way most people lead their lives.

Despite Mrs Thatcher's Victorian morals and the ravages of the recession over the last decade, a transformation in the relations between the sexes has been consolidated. This is not to say that there is now equality; far from it. Instead there has been an unfreezing of fixed relations in the family – some space for manoeuvre has opened up for women and children – and uncertainty has entered men's domestic lives. Much of this was set in motion by capitalism's need for new sources of labour, sucking women into the labour force during the years of economic expansion. But in gaining the freedoms and tyrannies of a wage packet on a scale unprecedented in history, women have begun to shift the centre of gravity in a whole series of social, educational and cultural spheres.

Looking back at the years when the momentum for change seemed greatest – in the late 1960s and early 1970s – much of what was happening sexually (now catalogued under the title 'the sexual revolution') seems more of an attempt by men to contain these changes, to bed the threat. Much of the spirit of that time – whilst it was about breaking out of the deadly embrace of the nuclear family – also seems to have been so compulsive about sex as to suggest that its agenda was set by men, and that progress was dominated by men's sexual anxieties. This book, in one way, is a throwback to the years before the 1960s. It is not about how to be a better lover or have bigger orgasms. It goes back to some of the words and ideas – like intimacy and vulnerability – which don't sit easily with 60s notions of pleasure and sensation freed from the 'oppressive' ties of love and romance. Those days have passed, but at least one of their products has gone on to prosper and expand – the porn industry.

Andy Moye, in chapter 4, writes about the exchange of services – the man providing the finance, the woman the physical and emotional care of the home – which underlay the typical marriage in the past. This exchange was not a cold-blooded barter in the market place. For one thing, it was an unequal exchange, and for another the family was the place for warmth, feeling and belonging. The only way the structured inequality in this exchange could be mediated and tolerated was if women complied with their own relative lack of power in the world, and were satisfied by holding emotional power in the home. When fissures and cracks started to appear in this delicately-balanced kingdom, when more and more women began to renounce their complicity, the search was on for substitutes who would comply with the exercise of male power. Andy Moye argues that the power pornography exerts over men stems largely from this history. He describes pornography in such a way that it appears both strikingly silent about the complexities of male desire, but also infantile in the way it relentlessly manipulates images of subordinated women.

This is only one of the instances in this book, where the two underlying themes of the collection come together. We think that future work on sexuality would benefit from further integrating these approaches – exploring the way gender orders 'object relations' and thus the unconscious. Neither approach on its own can begin to grasp the sense which also pervades this book – that of a past which seems to be colliding against, or slipping through the present, a hallucination of time, which we men seem to embrace avidly. A framework which retains a materialist stance and focuses on the relationship of social change to internal and unconscious motivations can grasp the contradictions and paradoxes of human sexuality.

Away from the home and the bedroom, in the arena of public politics, masculinity has been played upon to devastating effect. In the popularization of a monetarist economic policy on both sides of the Atlantic, care has been taken to present these strategies as being proper to the competitive instincts of red-blooded American and British males. The call goes out to kill off lame ducks, to forswear compassion. It is asserted that in the market place only the fittest should survive, and that a hard, lean industrial sector is necessary. Appeals to machismo and to disdain soft emotions are quite naked, as politicians of the radical right pour scorn on the need to care for the less fortunate, on the whole idea of a welfare state. In social policy, Mrs Thatcher has lost no opportunity in stressing the importance of voluntary charitable work – provided it is done by women – and at the same time she has steadily cut back the safety net of the welfare state. My concern here is not with the actual case for a monetarist solution but with the imagery, and the implicit messages concerning gender, which have imbued and fortified this onslaught from the right.

Although the gaining of the leadership of the Tory party by Mrs Thatcher was, in one sense a tribute to the weakening of gender division, her style of politics as well as the overt policy measures she has presided over, seem motivated in part by a need to shore up the imperatives of gender division: to remind women where their place is – by their man – and to kick some bottle into the men. In part, the continuing hold her politics have over a substantial section of the British population stems from her own particular determination to deal with the politics of gender. It has been easier for Mrs Thatcher to do this by implication than it has in policy terms. The dropping of the extreme manifesto by the Cabinet's 'family policy group' indicates that room for manoeuvre on family policy is limited. Despite this, Mrs Thatcher, through her style, and mastery of TV interviewers, manages to weave into any topic a commentary – in subliminal terms – about modern masculinity and femininity. This is partly because the whole thrust of Thatcherite politics is to promise that through a hard, resolute approach, there will be an end to Britain's decline. These politics are able to exploit the sense of public unease about the benefits of the last thirty years of 'progress' during which Britain's place in the world has slipped steadily.

Ironically, what persists and lingers in these forays is a powerful, if understated, commentary on gender's changing boundaries. It's partly the blend of high moral tone and machismo and partly the bald fact that a woman is in charge. But in the appeal to old certainties, it all in the end adds up to a hymn to the patriarchial, imperial sensibilities of the audience, a balm to male anxieties.

In the USA and Britain growing western militarism has played on the most reactionary ideas of male sexuality. Adverts in armaments magazines show bullets glossily painted to look like lipsticks; guns and missiles are given the sheen of the all-conquering phallus. Links are created between military strategies and masculine attitudes as the media establishes a visual format which correlates the occupation of land with the occupation of women's bodies.

To the general public, President Reagan and Mrs Thatcher sell themselves as military leaders, the leaders of fighting men, real men, not wimps and wets. This is boy's stuff, the right stuff, and, as the Falklands war showed, it has remarkable power. A war fought at considerable cost, with significant casualties, for a few bleak, scarcely-populated islands with a lot of sheep, was enough to reverse the Conservative Party's slump in popularity and win them the 1983 general election. This was no mean feat – and it was largely due to the symbolic meanings attached to going to war. Churchillian phrases dripped from the mouths of the 'War Cabinet', as a sordid xenophobic enterprise was transformed into a paean to manhood, a celebration of the phallus draped in the Union Jack. Resurgent nationalism and a refurbished manhood were fused into one as the ships left port, the jets screamed overhead, and wives and sweethearts cried and waved goodbye. Everyone was in their place. We'd seen the movie a hundred times: now it was time for the real thing.

The quite different sense of power which the women of Greenham Common have exercised also originates from a willingness to engage with the *real* issue of men and male sexuality. Greenham Common is a worldwide symbol of the struggle against militarism not just because of the extraordinary determination of the women, but also because these women have made it clear that they are not going to be left at home on the dockside to pick up the pieces when the men return. They have refused the role of passive possessions, for whom the men will risk all – in this case, the whole human race. They have made the equation between male power and militarism – and have refused to be complicit in the exercise of that power. In their struggle against the disturbed and distorted aspects of male sexuality on which militarism breeds, gender has been made an integral part of the movement for peace.

Sexuality, then, and particularly male sexuality as currently constructed, is not purely a private affair. It suffuses public life. It has been harnessed to work for political ends by the most reactionary forces in society. Men have a choice in this – they can continue to keep silent, keep holding on, and hope the cavalry arrives soon. The alternative starts with acknowledging our need to change, to articulate a sense that we can have a real and strong masculine identity without displaying the most desperate and violent attitudes towards women, and towards our own natures.

More and more men are discovering this, giving up some of the emptier poses of masculinity, and beginning to find themselves outside the oppressive structures which gender division creates in our society. These moves, in response to – as well as accepting – the challenge of feminism, are part of the struggle for liberation. They will not end conflicts between men and women, but they do point to ways of resolving conflicts which do not rely on the use of male physical or economic power. They also expose the myth, which the right plays on so readily, that at bottom, all men are big bad wolves. It is true that much male thinking is infused with misogyny – but that is neither unchanging or immutable. Beneath the mask of manly resolve there is all too often a chaotic state of conflict and ambivalence, constantly alluded to, but rarely allowed to escape. But there is nothing inevitable about this. As the boundary lines of gender division have become more and more blurred, so men have begun to change. And this hasn't been a dreary wet course in learning feminist orthodoxy by rote: the price of becoming a man and wielding relative power over women (and other men) has become apparent. This book offers an alternative vision of men and their sexuality. A vision based on the possibilities of change. But for this to be more than words, confessions or good intentions, for it to be a living process, it requires men to end their state of silence.

2. Roots of masculinity

What are little girls made of?
Sugar and spice and all things nice,
That's what little girls are made of.
What are little boys made of?
Slugs and snails and puppy dogs' tails,
That's what little boys are made of.

Well not exactly; but even though it's crude the nursery rhyme reflects what everybody already knows: that there is an obvious difference between the sexes, including a qualitative difference in the psychological experience of being female, as femininity, and being male, as masculinity. Less obvious is the complex process by which each individual comes to establish his or her gender identity.

From the increased studies of sexuality and gender identity over the past two decades, it has become apparent that many more men than women experience problems about their gender identity. As a psychotherapist, I have increasingly observed from my clinical practice that men, in varying degrees, are either confused or in conflict about their sense of masculinity. There is reason to believe that the intersexed nature of the mother son relationship is a key to the understanding of men's fragile gender identity and the related problems of fear of commitment and intimacy. In this essay, I discuss the psychological roots of masculinity by focusing on the developmental process towards establishing a gender identity which leads to problems in intimate relationships, dependency and autonomy.

An essential part of how we define and order ourselves in the world is through our sense of being male or female, our sexual or gender identity. Both biological and psychological factors contribute to gender differentiation, but exactly what part each plays, and to what degree, is the subject of a highly controversial debate on the age-old 'nature/nurture' problem.[1]

Caught between the complexities of the process of sexual differentiation, and the hazardous route towards consolidation of gender identity, it is not surprising that most, if not all, individuals experience some confusion about their sense of gender. What needs further exploration is the fact that many more men than women experience serious problems regarding their gender identity. For example, transexualism – where the individual feels that he or she is really a member of the opposite sex and has a persistent wish to change sex anatomically – is prevalent in a significantly greater proportion of males than females. Fetishistic cross-dressing or transvestism – the compulsive desire to cross-dress for the purpose of sexual arousal and sexual pleasure – is exclusively practised by males. Many more men than women engage in perversions – sexual practices that are compulsive, preferred and necessary for full satisfaction; for example, fetishism, voyeurism, exhibitionism and necrophilia are exclusively male activities. Even masochism, which is widely considered by many psychoanalysts as an inherent part of femininity, is in fact actively pursued as a sexual practice by more men than women.

As a psychotherapist, I continually meet and work with men who present a variety of psychological problems, but they all have in common to varying degrees a deep concern about their masculinity. One frequent manifestation of this is a preoccupation with the size of their penis. This is not just a worry about an anatomical reality, but reflects a deeper psychological insecurity about maleness as symbolised by the penis. Some men distort their perceptions of their penis, reducing the actual size to equate with a diminished view of themselves as male.

One young man I know was completely disorientated and

baffled upon realizing during a sexual encounter that his penis was larger than he had previously believed. Another man experiences his penis as small and shrivelled. Besides being dissociated from his penis, believing it to have a 'mind of its own', he experiences difficulty urinating in public toilets. One day, while urinating with more ease than usual, he experienced his penis becoming 'stronger, more fleshy, as if it were more real'. A moment later he thought something 'terrible' or 'horrific' was about to happen. For a short moment he had a glimpse of what it might be like to feel integrated in his body and to acknowledge and confirm his sense of maleness. It is not uncommon to hear of men who continually, but secretly, compare the size of their penis with others. Obviously this measure is an attempt to confirm their sense of being a man.

Sometimes the whole body, or parts of the body other than the genitalia, are distorted. One young man recounted to me that he refused to expose his arms in public for fear that he would appear weak and feminine. Yet another man believes that his fair complexion and sparse body hair is evidence that he is more female than male.

A more blatant form of gender insecurity and distortion is expressed through the wish to dress as a woman or the wish to be a woman. Transvestism and transexualism are the extreme examples of this. I believe many men harbour such wishes which appear in dreams, fantasies and on occasion may be enacted, for instance, at carnivals or costume parties. A cultural manifestation of this is seen in the contemporary pop scene with its interest in androgenous cult figures. Other examples of men wishing to be women or turning into women are to be found in mythology. Besides indicating a lack of firmness in men's sense of their masculinity, these examples also strongly suggest men's envy of women, particularly expressed through the wish to be a woman.

Freud was the first to offer a dynamic and comprehensive theory of sexual identity.[2] For him, masculinity and femininity develop out of the special conflict and resolution known as the Oedipus complex. Boys, he argued, begin life with an advantage over girls in that their love object is heterosexual. During the oedipal phase, the attachment to the mother becomes sexualized, while the father looms large as a rival. Under threat of punishment (castration) the boy must give up his mother as a sexual object and identify with his father. Thus he preserves his heterosexuality and establishes his masculine identity. For the girl, the path towards femininity is less straightforward, with the added complication that her primary love object is of the same sex. To establish a heterosexual attachment she must continue to identify with the mother, while shifting her love from her mother to her father. Unlike the boy, the change of sexual object comes about through defeat i.e. she learns that she can never possess the mother because she lacks a penis. The change to the father is motivated by resentment because the little girl blames her mother for her inadequacy (lack of a penis) and the loss of the mother.

Findings from contemporary research challenge Freud's view in three major ways. Firstly, there is the supposition that gender identity is a consequence of early primary learning. According to Freud, gender is undifferentiated until the resolution of the Oedipus complex at around three to five years of age. Boys and girls are considered the same i.e. masculine, until the girl recognises the lack of a penis, thus realizing her femininity. Ordinary observation alone can provide evidence that children, well before the age of three, know the difference between the sexes. Even children a year old display kinesics and gestures appropriate to their sex as defined by cultural criteria.

Secondly, there is the supposition that the gender of a child is differentiated and discernible well before the Oedipal phase. This is the most controversial challenge to Freud's theory of sexual identity, and of course, to all biologically determined theories. Robert Stoller,[3] like John Money, believes that gender differentiation begins at birth when parents and midwife assign the child its sex. What sex the parents believe the child to be will greatly influence its gender identity. The knowledge about their infants' genitals will affect, consciously and unconsciously, the parents' attitude, manner of holding, speaking to, and interacting with the infant. Parental confusions about their own gender or their unresolved hostility towards the opposite sex may cause future gender problems for their own children.

Stoller believes that this type of direct learning is similar to 'imprinting', a concept borrowed from ethology which describes a type of primary learning in which the central nervous system is directly affected and thereby affects subsequent behaviour. This is a conflict-free area of learning which results in the term Stoller coined as the 'core identity', a basic sense of self, either male or female. It is the base from which masculinity or femininity is constructed; and established around eighteen months, it cannot be reversed. Even with severe psychological distress such as psychosis or organic brain damage, the individual will continue to experience him or herself according to the core identity – either as male or female – although there may be conflict or confusion about the degree to which individuals experience themselves as masculine or feminine. Core identity is an essential experience of being fixed in one's sex, whereas femininity and masculinity are expressions of what one learns to be expected behaviour of someone who is female or male.

Thirdly, there is the supposition that masculinity, not femininity, is the weaker of the gender constructs. Freud's view that femininity is failed masculinity has been criticized from the very beginning. More recent research continues to take up the challenge. Even on the biological level, it is now known that we all begin life as a female foetus. To differentiate the foetus as male, something must be added – testosterone, the male hormone. During this process of differentiation much can go awry. Of all the intersex disorders studied by John Money a larger proportion were genetically male than were female.[4] But one need not resort to biology for a causal explanation of the male's seemingly fragile gender identity. The psychological explanation may be analogous to the biological in that 'something must be added' for the boy to establish his masculinity. Freud's view that boys were at an advantage over girls because their primary love object is heterosexual is based on anatomy, rather than identity. If identity is taken as the reference point, it is the boy who experiences more difficulties with gender differentiation. In order for him to establish masculinity he must first dis-identify from his mother, and then identify with his father.[5] The girl's route to femininity is more straightforward, as her primary identification is with someone of the same sex – her mother.

All infants begin life in a primitive symbiotic relationship with the mother or surrogate mother. The eventual task of development is to differentiate oneself from one's mother and to become a separate individual. Commensurate with its physical growth, the infant develops psychological capacities which enable it to differentiate between similarities and contrasts, and to discriminate between 'inside' and 'outside'. Eventually the child becomes aware of the difference between outside objects, including its mother and others, and itself, thus enabling it to be aware of self and non-self. At the same time the child is learning to differentiate between others and itself, it is also modelling itself on the mother i.e. identifying with the mother. The various fundamental tasks such as walking, talking and holding objects are learned, in fact, through intimation of the primary caring person, the mother. Of course, the imitation is modified by the child's mental and physical endowment. Thus identification with the mother is the beginning of identity and the basis from which later identifications are formed. What is important to our understanding of male gender identity is that in order for a boy to develop masculinity, he must first give up his identification with his mother and identify with his father. This task is further complicated and made difficult because the boy may not wish to give up the 'security given closeness' that identification with the mother provides.

Several factors can impede this process of disidentification. The mother may not wish to give up the hold she has on her son because of her own difficulties in defining herself as a separate individual, or she may be confused and ambivalent about her own gender. She may experience her son as an extension of herself, and thereby exclude any expression of autonomy or masculinity from him. According to Stoller mothers of transexuals feminize their sons through their insistence of a special and close relationship which excludes and denies any hint of difference.[6]

If the mother is hostile, consciously or unconsciously, towards men in general or the father in particular, this may greatly affect the boy's move away from the mother and his capacity to identify with the father. In this type of situation the difference between mother and son is not denied but it is attacked so that the boy finds it difficult to experience himself as male without confusion, self-doubt and self-loathing. In the extreme, this is the dynamic present in the family of the transvestite, particularly if the boy has been punished in the past by being forced to dress up in girl's clothing. In less extreme cases there is no cross-dressing but the boy's gender identity is negatively affected.

It is most important to stress that it is not just the mother who is responsible for the boy's difficulties with establishing masculinity. In our culture it is mainly women who take care of children and this presents special difficulties for boys in their development; but fathers can also play a significant role in this process. If the father is absent, or inaccessible when he is present, this may impede the boy's separation from the mother and the identification with his father. Fathers who are cold, distant or aggressive erect barriers against the boy's identification with them. This is particularly the case where actual bodily harm is done to the mother or son. Of course, fathers who are ambivalent or confused about their own sexual identity may find it hard to support their son in establishing his masculinity.

The experience of being reared by someone of the opposite sex has further consequences for the male. Fears of commitment or dependency in relationships, sometimes experienced as fear of entrapment, may be linked to the male's cross-identification with his mother. These fears, which are more common among males than females, feature in varying degrees amongst men from the so-called normal to the more emotionally disturbed. In my own clinical practice I would say that most, if not all, the men I meet exhibit some fear of closeness or intimacy with women. Sometimes this is manifested by complete exclusion of the woman from their lives or in less extreme cases the man may behave in ways to curtail, control or distance himself within the relationship. The aim is to ensure continuous control in relation to a woman in order to diminish the threat of her overwhelming powers.

Most therapists, as well as most women (being the feared objects), have frequently heard complaints from men about fears of being dominated, controlled, swallowed up or suffocated. Underlying these fears, which on the surface appear to be concerned with autonomy and freedom, is a more basic fear about the disintegration or loss of their sense of maleness. Behind this fear appears to be the wish to surrender to the woman, to be like her, to be in union with her. It may be that these fears and wishes are present in all men, but certainly they are clearly observed in men who demonstrate phobic behaviour towards women.

The following clinical example illustrates these points. Dave, a thirty year old professional man, came to therapy because of his inability to commit himself to a relationship without feeling anxious and fearful. According to him, when demands for commitment were made of him, he retreated, fearing that he would be controlled or swallowed up by his partner. His most recent relationship actually survived for several years, but repeated discord and separations left him feeling lonely, depressed and despairing. Away from his partner he felt love and affection for her, but while with her, especially during moments of intimacy, he experienced feelings of irritation and anxiety. A pattern developed whereby when he felt entrapped he behaved in a contemptuous or rejecting manner, inducing his partner to reject and leave him. The pattern of rejection, separation and reconciliation was repeated innumerable times until Dave's partner finally decided to disengage herself from the relationship. Dave is attracted, for what at first seem to be aesthetic reasons, to women of 'angular and athletic' build. He wishes his partners to be 'firm and sharp'. In other words there must be no hint of softness or largeness, particularly in the breasts – what Dave calls 'the motherly type'. On occasions when Dave has seen or been with a 'fat' or 'large' woman, he experiences a sensation of being lost or enveloped by their 'layers of flesh'. I believe what Dave fears most is his own wish to be enveloped, to be lost in the woman. All of his attempts to order and control his perceptions and behaviour, as well as those of his partners, are in the service of checking his own desires to be abandoned to a woman. A fear and a wish exist simultaneously.

As with all men who fear intimacy with women, Dave is obsessed with concerns about his masculinity. Even though his appearance and build does not strongly deviate from what is culturally considered to be masculine, he believes himself to be weak and small, a poor specimen of a man. He is plagued by the need to 'prove himself' but always fears that he could never measure up to, or defend himself from, attack. As a child, Dave experienced his father and his brother as strong and aggressive. Family loyalty was highly regarded, it being understood that the men would defend the family against outside attack. Aggression was condoned, even encouraged. If Dave retreated from battles with other boys, his father or brother would force him to fight again. There was nothing worse than a coward, except perhaps, a boy who was a 'sissy'. Dave was considered a 'sissy' by his father and brother because of his close relationship with his mother. He enjoyed doing things with her, and he appeared to have identified with her temperament and interests. Dave's sense of protectiveness towards his mother against his father's aggressive outbursts seemed to reinforce the already existing close bond between mother and son.

Sometimes fear of intimacy is so great that some men employ measures to ensure that they will never find themselves in that situation. For example, Ralph, a twenty-two year old student, is preoccupied most of his waking days with the thought of becoming intimate with a woman. His attempts to meet women are thwarted by what he believes to be fears of rejection. He considered himself to be ugly and unmanly, he thinks that he does not have what it takes and that the rules of courtship elude him. To avoid rejection he must ascertain with certainty that the woman is reciprocally attracted to him, so he scrutinizes her every word and gesture to discover clues of interest. Of course, he never finds this certainty but continues to lead a life of misery, despairing from the fear of repeated rejections by women.

Obviously, Ralph does suffer from fears of rejection, but I believe that these fears are part of a self-deception to protect himself from the greater fear – intimacy, particularly sexual intimacy. On occasion, Ralph has acknowledged these fears which are experienced in terms of being controlled, taken over and dominated. Like Dave, Ralph is also preoccupied with his sense of maleness. He considers himself small and skinny, which is an obvious self-distortion as his work with weights has helped him to develop an athletic build.

A collusion has developed between Ralph and his mother, whereby he continually confides in her about his failures with women and she responds by proffering reassurance and advice, which he in turn devalues and resents. Obviously Ralph blames his mother for his feelings of inadequacy or lack of masculinity and he wishes to induce feelings of guilt in her by parading his failures in front of her. However, he also appears to be continually reaffirming their love and closeness. If he fails with other women, their relationship continues. When younger, Ralph suffered from a speech defect manifested by a slight stammer. According to him, his mother 'read his mind'; she knew what he wanted to say and completed his sentences for him. Ralph feels trapped between his dependency on his mother and his experiences of her as controlling and dominating. This continues to keep him at home and strongly contributes to his fears of other possible intimate relationships.

Another manifestation of men's fears of intimacy with women is expressed through their attitude and behaviour towards the female body, especially the vagina. Many men in my therapy practice have recounted how the sight or touch of the vagina disgusts them. Some are completely phobic, refusing to touch or even look at the female genitalia. They regard the vagina as ugly, distasteful, smelly, a gaping hole. There is a fear of its foreignness. Traditionally, this has been interpreted as castration anxiety. The vagina is frightening or threatening because it reminds the man of what could happen to him: the loss of his penis. More is at stake than just the precious organ, for the threat of loss of the penis, the insignia of all that is maleness (masculinity), represents a fear of the disintegration of the self as a separate identity.

Behind the fear of the vagina as a castrating agent lies the threat that the sinister female genitalia will control or devour. For example, the vagina is not uncommonly referred to as a vice with an unyielding grip or a gaping hole which draws, sucks and devours the man. Perhaps this is the anxiety of men who suffer from premature ejaculation; if they visit too long they will become entrapped.

Here is a masturbation fantasy of a man I know. A woman binds him and forces him on his knees to perform cunnilingus. He is fearful and humiliated, yet excited. When with a woman sexually this is what he most wishes to do but dares not. Through the protectiveness of his fantasy, he gives in to his desire to surrender, to please, to be hers, an expression of the intimacy which he fears in his relationship. In non-fantasy relationships he constantly monitors and controls women, apparently because he fears domination by them but more accurately because he needs to check his own desire to surrender.

Thus far I have argued, contrary to Freud's view, that men's sense of their maleness (masculinity) is less secure than women's experience of their femininity. When one focuses on identity rather than anatomy, it becomes evident that men encounter unique problems due to the intersex nature of the mother son relationship. To develop masculinity, the boy first must dis-identify from his mother, but the primary identification with mother is never completely eradicated. It remains interwoven in the very core of what we call masculinity. Varying in degree with different individuals, this primary identity may exert a powerful pull.

Within the present context of child-rearing practice, I believe that Robert Stoller has it right when he states:

> . . . the whole process of becoming masculine is at risk in the little boy from the date of his birth on; his still-to-be-created masculinity is endangered by the primary, profound, primaeval oneness with the mother, a blissful experience that serves, buried but active in the core of one's identity, as a focus that, throughout life, can attract one to regress back to that primitive oneness, that is the threat lying latent in masculinity. I suggest the need to fight it off is what energizes some of what we are familiar with when we call a piece of behaviour 'masculine'.[7]

Masculinity, then, can be viewed as a defensive construction developed over the early years out of a need to emphasise a difference, a separateness from the mother. In the extreme this is manifested by machismo behaviour with its emphasis on competitiveness, strength, aggressiveness, contempt for women and emotional shallowness, all serving to keep the male secure in his separate identity. It may be that to appear 'weak' which many men wrongly associate with femininity, is also threatening to men because it lessens the psychological gap between the sexes.

Also, autonomy (more accurately a false sense of autonomy) is closely linked to the development of masculinity. To ensure a separateness many men deny feelings of need or dependency, finding them a threat to an already fragile identity. To indicate a need of or dependence on a woman for some men would be tantamount to self-annihilation. Such is the dilemma for men with their maleness and masculinity. To have a sense of separateness, a difference must be fortified and defended; hence the demonstration by many men of an exaggerated virility paraded as autonomy. Any expression of need or desire carries with it the threat of succumbing to a wish to be united with, or the same as, the woman. The ways and means by which each man resolves these issues of separation and identity will determine his capacity to risk himself in intimate relationships and to allow the expression of feelings and desires which hitherto have been feared and denied.

What effect would a change in present child-rearing practices have on the development and experience of male gender identity? At present women are still the predominant providers of primary care to children, but through feminism and the possibility of economic opportunities, many more women have redefined themselves, left the home and entered the workforce. Also, more men, by necessity or desire, are actively participating in the early care and nurturing of their children. Exactly how this will affect the boy's sense of maleness is difficult to say, but it could well be that a redefinition of parental roles will lessen the need for the defensive posturing inherent in masculinity. As women gain real power, the need for self-validation attained exclusively through their nurturing role with their children will be diminished, thus enabling mother and son to give up the 'security given closeness' and to separate with less drama and struggle. The active presence and participation of fathers in the early nurturing of their children may provide a less defensive, softer model of masculinity. Primary identification with the mother will still exist but rather than being feared and denied, it will come to be accepted and appreciated.

3. Male sexuality in the media

One would think that writing about images of male sexuality would be as easy as anything. We live in a world saturated with images, drenched in sexuality. But this is one of the reasons why it is in fact difficult to write about. Male sexuality is a bit like air – you breathe it in all the time, but you aren't aware of it much. Until quite recently, what was talked about was the mysterious topic of female sexuality, or else, the subject of deviant male sexual practices. Ordinary male sexuality was simply sexuality, and everybody knew what it was. As I'll be arguing later, we look at the world through ideas of male sexuality. Even when not looking *at* male sexuality, we are looking at the world within its terms of reference.

Given the range and pervasiveness of imagery of male sexuality in the media, I have decided to concentrate on three specific aspects: the visual symbols for it, the treatment of it in comedy, and the way it informs the telling of stories. These aspects lie behind the very varied images of male sexuality that the media throw up – they are part of a sexual grammar that underlies and structures the vast majority of representations of male sexuality. The first and last aspects – symbols and storytelling – are so routine that they feel almost natural, just 'the way things are done'; and by seeming so obvious and inevitable, we can lose sight of the fact that what they are actually representing is a particular sense of male sexuality, with its own history and social form. Comedy too may reproduce these seemingly natural ideas of human sexuality, but it is contradictory as well, often exploding the myths of male sexuality by raising a laugh. These then are the topics I shall be covering, drawing my examples mainly from film and television, but also occasionally from other visual media.

The symbolism of male sexuality

Outside pornography, sexuality, male or female, is not so much shown directly as symbolized. It is not just censorship that insists on this – sexuality is on the whole better represented through symbolism. Colours, textures, objects, effects of light, the shape of things, all this and more is given through evocation, resonance and association; these set off feelings about what sex is like more efficiently than just showing acts of sex. Pornography too uses the devices of symbolism to construct a particular sense of the sex it shows. What is significant is how sexuality is symbolized, how these devices evoke a sense of what sexuality is like, how they contribute to a particular definition of sexuality.

The first thing to say about the symbolism of male sexuality is that it is overwhelmingly centred on the genitals, especially the penis. Penises are not shown, but the evocation of male sexuality is almost always an evocation of the penis. Male sexuality is repeatedly equated with the penis; men's sexual feelings are rendered as somehow being 'in' their penises. Sexual arousal in women, where it is represented at all, may use a plethora of indications – arching bodies, undulating shoulders, hands caressing breasts, hips, arms, textures and surfaces that suggest all this – such is the vocabulary of female desire in the media. With men, the symbolism implies the erect penis. Mae West's famous gag, 'Is that a gun in your pocket or are you just pleased to see me?', characteristically goes straight to the point, that male pleasure in seeing a woman will be visibly registered in the penis; that male sexual pleasure is seen to happen in the penis. The list of objects that have been used as penis symbols is endless – trains going into tunnels, cigars raised from the lips, guns held close to the hips, and so on *ad nauseam*. However, there is no other accepted symbol of male arousal, even though we know that many zones of the male body are erogenous. Even when other parts of the male body are used to represent sexuality it is only because they can symbolize the penis, as in the commonest symbol of them all, the fist raised from the elbow.

One of the striking characteristics about penis symbols is the discrepancy between the symbols and what penises are actually like. Male genitals are fragile, squashy, delicate things; even when erect, the penis is spongy, seldom straight, and rounded at the tip, while the testicles are imperfect spheres, always vulnerable, never still. There are very exceptional cases where something of the exquisiteness and softness of the male genitals is symbolized. Constance Beeson, in her film of male gay love, uses the imagery of the flower's stamen (*Stamen* is the title of her film), to evoke the male genitals. Jean Genet, in his writings and his film, *Un Chant d'Amour*, also uses flowers to symbolize the penis, and writes of an erection being like a flower unfolding. In a particularly delicate film scene he uses the image of a straw pushed through a wall (in the prison where the film is set), with one man blowing smoke through it into the mouth of another – the thin, easily broken straw, the gentle wisps of smoke, these are blatant but soft images of the penis and semen in fellatio. Such imagery also suggests that male genitals can be thought of as beautiful, and there are instances of male nude painting and photography which do treat the genitals as if they are something lovely to look at – for instance, Sylvia Sleigh's gently ironic paintings, or the tradition of gay male photography that deliberately evokes classical antiquity. Yet such examples are marginal. Far more commonly the soft, vulnerable charm of male genitals is evoked as hard, tough, and dangerous. It is not flowers that most commonly symbolize male genitals but swords, knives, fists, guns.

One of the steamiest images of male sexual arousal in the cinema occurs near the beginning of the classic Japanese film *Rashomon*. The warrior, played by Toshiro Mifune, lies half-naked and unshaven under a tree. A beautiful woman passes by escorted by her husband. Mifune does not move, but his eyes stare at her off-screen, and gradually the sword that is dangling over his knee rises up at an angle to his body. A hard, gleaming weapon is at once understood to be like a penis; impossible to imagine flower imagery being used as a prelude to this tale of rape and seduction.

Yet even erect the penis and testicles are not hard, tough, weapon-like. The penis cannot stab and do all the other violent things it is evoked as being capable of, for fear of being hurt itself by doing so; even in rape, it is the humiliation, and the other actual weapons used, that do more damage than the penis itself. Moreover, the penis is also the symbol of male potency, the magic and mystery of the phallus, the endowment that appears to legitimate male power. Yet penises are only little things (even big ones) without much staying power, pretty if you can learn to see them like that, but not magical or mysterious or powerful in themselves, that is, not objectively full of real power.

Such visual symbolism not only reduces male sexuality to the penis, cutting us off from other erotic pleasures, and placing on the penis a burden of being driving, tough, aggressive, it also tends to separate men from their sexuality. The penis is seen to have a life of its own, leading the man on almost despite himself. At best the man is seen as the possessor or owner of this object, but it is an object over which he does not have full control. It is the beast below.

The idea of the penis, and hence of male sexuality, as separable from the man, forms the basis of stories about male sexuality, especially those with a violent or bestial view of sexual intercourse itself. Pursuit, seduction, rape, murder – not only are these different story events hard to distinguish from each other, not only do the bellicose symbols of male sexuality so easily lend themselves to the representation of sexuality as violence, but also the sense of the penis-weapon being apart from the man often absolves him of responsibility for his actions. It is not the man that is being aggressive, it is his penis. Even stories of rape and murder that do not seek to make a hero of the rapist/murderer (as many do), that present acts of rape and murder as repulsive (and not the turn-on that so many representations suggest these acts as), that do not seek to blame women, these nonetheless suggest that the man can't help it – it was his *penis* that did it.

This excuse for rape really pulls together two arguments. Firstly, it does not distinguish between power/domination and sexuality; it explains male power over women in terms of sexuality, a sexuality habitually symbolized in terms of weaponry and aggressive drive. Acts of power and domination, such as rape and murder, are seen as acts of sexuality. Since sexuality is supposedly natural, acts that express it can be viewed as pre-social and irresponsible because they are beyond social or individual responsibility. Secondly, the idea of the separateness of male sexuality 'it's all happening down there' leads to accepting the natural irresponsibility of men; but what I want to stress here is the habitual seeing of male sexuality as separate, down there, apart, not a part. It may be that the given physiology of male and female genitals – men's hanging down away from the body, women's tucked up inside it – is the last resort of this argument. Women are somehow connected to their sexuality in a way that men are not. We don't have to make sense of our different sexualities in this way, but the given visible difference has certainly suited patriarchial arguments that men 'can't help' having bestial desires.

The most common imagery of male sexuality, then, focuses on the penis as the locus of male sexuality, and sees the penis in a particular way – down there, hard, importunate. This is an extraordinarily constricted and ugly way of imagining the erotic, which makes it difficult to portray male sexual experience in terms of tenderness and beauty. It is also very tough, serious and po faced, which is why you can't help wanting to giggle at it sometimes, and why it is such a rich source of comedy.

Comedy

Sex comedy is one of the artistic forms (horror stories are

another) that consistently plays on ambivalences surrounding male sexuality, some of them stemming from the symbolism I've just been discussing. Comedy is an area of expression that is licensed to explore aspects of life that are difficult, contradictory and distressing. I don't mean to imply that comedy is inherently subversive, but simply to suggest that comedy can get away with making fun of things that other genres with a more straight-faced attitude cannot. Popular comedy tends particularly to exploit the contradictory nature of things, of attitudes, precisely because it aims to be popular, to appeal to different people with different attitudes. If a gag or a sketch can gather together these different contradictory attitudes it will be more popular, if only in the numerical sense of appealing to more people.

Comedy is then fertile terrain for considering images of sexuality. I want to look here at explicit, even crude, sex comedy: seaside postcards, *Carry On* films, the American sex comedies of the fifties and sixties (for instance, *The Seven Year Itch, The Girl Can't Help It, Pillow Talk*), TV sitcoms such as *George and Mildred, Are You Being Served?* and *Hi-De-Hi!*, and comedians such as Frankie Howerd and Benny Hill. Much of this humour plays on the anxiety caused by the gap between what male genitals are actually like and what they are supposed to be like. Humour can touch on male fears about the inability to live up to what penises claim for them and can endorse female derision about the patriarchial overestimation of the penis.

There is, for instance, a seaside postcard which shows (from behind) a muscleman holding a barbell aloft; he is surrounded by kneeling, bikini-clad, nubile women; his trunks have slipped off round his thighs. The gag line is 'It's magnificent, but he can't keep it up for five minutes.' All the women are staring fixedly at the man's penis; the expressions on their faces flatter male estimation of the effect the sight of male genitals has on women, namely awe and delight. However, the man's expression is not of sexual pride but embarrassment at having been revealed; his is the standard male face in seaside postcards, bright red, snub-nosed, a face normally associated with the hen-pecked, feckless male. And the gag line greatly deflates male pride, hitting on one of the great male fears about penetration and sex, that of not being able to keep it going, not staying hard.

Much sexual comedy plays on the idea of the penis apart from the man, leading him on into mischief, making a fool of him. Such comedy can both ridicule men, subject them to indignities, and it also validates the idea of male sexuality as essentially asocial, outside of social construction and responsibility. The British comedy film *Percy* deals with a shy man who, as a result of an accident, has to have a penis transplant; the donor is a randy womanizer. With this new penis, Percy finds that, despite his modest reserve, he is constantly running after women, led on by his genitals. His penis doesn't belong to him, it is importunate, he can't help himself. It's a sharp, comic idea, although in the event, a dreary movie.

The apparent butt of sexual comedy is often a woman – yet, as so often with images of women, the joke is often really about men. Two female types are particularly common – the harridan and the busty blonde. The first symbolizes male hostility to women; the latter on the other hand seems primarily concerned with exposing male weakness.

Among the more familiar incarnations of the harridan are the fat women from comic postcards, the dame in pantomime, and more recently, Mildred in the TV comedy *George and Mildred*. We are asked to laugh at her on three accounts. Firstly there is simply the fact that she is ugly – mounds of flesh for the postcard woman; excessive, strident make-up and hair-dos for the dame; and for Mildred, the cruel distortion of Yootha Joyce's portrayal. Then secondly, despite being ugly, she offers herself as attractive – the tiny polka-dot hat atop the fat woman of the postcards; the brilliant colours, elaborate gowns and peekaboo underclothes of the dame; the bright hair-dye and even brighter lipstick for Mildred. So, we are to laugh because they are not attractive, and then because they come on as if they are. A quintessential scene that brings these two elements together is the trying on of the slipper in any production of *Cinderella*, where the Ugly Sisters (as they are unabashedly called) primp up their stick-out bosoms, pucker their wildly misshapen lips and flutter their outrageously enormous eyelashes at a condescendingly amused Prince Charming. All the pretences of presentation that society wishes on women are here seen as coming from women as self-deceiving narcissism, all the more vicious, in *Cinderella*, for being practised at the expense of a poor, innocent – and, of course, beautiful – young girl. We can turn this comedy inside out and see that it expresses male resentment at finding women sexually arousing, male jealousy that it is women who are allowed to present themselves with such allure. Yet this tradition of humour never says as much. We have to bring such a view from outside the humour.

There is a third, related reason why the harridan is supposed to be funny, and that is because she's randy and predatory. The whole gag about Mildred is that she wanted sex, a want that poor little George could not satisfy. Harridans do not have to be grotesque to be funny; it is enough for them to be sexually alert. Ruth Madoc in *Hi-De-Hi!* is neat, pretty and smart, yet her constant desire for men makes her a comic terror. Here again we can see comedy working its magic, turning terror into laughter; but we have to work harder to see that the image of the comic expresses male fears and anxieties about female sexual energy, about the way it may test virility, about the way it challenges male supremacy.

Comedy that uses the image of the nubile, large-bosomed blonde woman only in part laughs at this figure of fun. Jayne Mansfield, Barbara Windsor and the string of performers featured in Benny Hill's shows are often at the centre of gags concerned with the extraordinary impact on men of overwhelming, uncontrollable sexual arousal. When Mansfield walks down the street in *The Girl Can't Help It*, a man unloading a huge block of ice finds it turning to steam in his hands – her impact just turns him red hot. The image that most immediately evokes British farce is a man with his trousers round his ankles wearing undershorts with brightly coloured, silly motifs upon them. The narrative that has led to this is nearly always the man's inability to stop himself, to stop his penis, from running after 'girls'. Benny Hill's whole act is a constant state of gleeful arousal – he is the man from the seaside postcard personified, round-faced, red-cheeked, snub-nosed. His clothes are always foolish, they never enhance or dignify his body, but coarsen and vulgarize it. And he spends all his time ogling or chasing women, no matter what he is supposed to be doing. Many sketches are simply built around him starting off doing something and being instantly, ineluctably, catastrophically, but delightedly, distracted by a bouncily-bosomed blonde woman passing by. Benny Hill in pursuit of women is never anything other than foolish to look at, and this is often accompanied by visual gags where paint brushes, lollipops or whatever are used as symbols of the eager and ridiculous penis.

Such perpetual randiness (of the little man in the seaside postcards, or Benny Hill, or George Formby or Sid James) robs men of any claim to be taken seriously, but also embraces grotty physicality as the stuff of life. It was in terms like these that George Orwell defended the seaside postcard in his article on the postcard artist, Donald McGill. Orwell suggested that postcard humour is an acknowledgement that life is not ideal, that sexual dreams and fantasies are only part of our make-up, that we also all know life to be mucky, awkward and scrappy, that sex especially is tacky. The image of male sexuality in postcards and comedy films is a welcome acceptance and embrace of the shortcomings of life, and Orwell is right to suggest that comedy can teach us a kind of robust, cheery recognition that sex (and all other facets of physical existence) falls far short of our ideals. Yet there are problems with this view of human sexual frailty. It celebrates sexual grottiness as if it were a permanent feature of the human condition; it promotes acceptance of male sexual failure in concert with derogatory and spiteful views of female sexuality; and its own itchy, tetchy squeamishness is itself a product of a society which loathes the human body.

Comedy is unruly – it can no more be secured for the right-on then it can for the right-wing. In comedy we see now a reinforcement of ideas expressed by the imagery of male sexuality, and now an undermining of them. What there isn't (at least, I can't think of an example) is comedy which shows that male sexuality need not be importunate, uncontrollable and quietly exhausted. Most comedy does in the end insist that, no matter how absurd male sexuality may be, that is what it is like. Comedy may often undermine men through ridiculing their sexuality, but it always ends up asserting as natural the prevalent social definition of that sexuality.

Male sexual narrative

So far I've been concentrating on how male sexuality is represented through male characters, performers and visual imagery. But the most insistent and relentless representation of male sexuality is not in how men are represented at all; but rather in the way that women are looked at by the camera eye. The very basic methods that film and television have developed for telling stories imply a particular sense of what male sexuality is. I am not talking here of the way that films centre on male protagonists whom we are all invited to identify with, and whose (generally sexist) attitudes to women we are supposed to share – though this is certainly a major feature of most media stories. Nor am I considering the way that narratives are structured around sexuality as pursuit, the man chasing the woman, that type of narrative that elides love, seduction, possession and rape. What I want to focus on here is the formal organization of storytelling – any story, not just an overtly sexual one – that reinforces a notion of male sexuality. I'll end by talking about the overall structure of narratives, but I'd like first to look at the way that we are invited to enter the fictional world of the story from scene to scene so as to see things from the male point of view, and moreover to see things through a particular sexual sensibility, that of the dominant notion of male sexuality. Much of the pleasure on offer depends on our experience of all kinds of sequences through this male sexuality. I want here to describe and discuss two of the most standard sequences in popular entertainment film and television – the 'heroine in jeopardy' sequence, and the 'lovers' first meeting' scene.

First, the heroine in jeopardy. In a horror film she has perhaps left her bedroom at night because she's heard a noise, she goes wandering through the twisting corridors of the gothic mansion anxiously holding aloft her guttering candle. In a thriller, she's perhaps gone visiting in a block of flats, one which happens to hide a psychopath on the run. The person she's gone to visit isn't there, and there's no one else around; she can't seem to open the front door and doesn't know what to do when the psychopath hears her rattling at the door. Or in a science fiction series, peak time *Dr Who* for instance, everyone is running to get away from the monster, whatever it is, and the heroine trips; she catches her ankle and the monster gets nearer. In all these cases it is always a woman who is trapped, a woman without resources to help herself. Heroes in jeopardy do something about it; heroines don't. And the pleasure we are supposed to get from seeing these sequences is that of seeing a woman in peril. We're supposed to get off on her vulnerability, her hysteria, her terror. In the way such sequences are put together, we are encouraged to take up a traditional male role in relation to the woman, one that asserts our superiority and at the same time encourages us to feel the desire to rape and conquer. We are superior because we either know more than her (we know that psychopath is there but she hasn't spotted him yet), or because we can see what any sensible person would do but she, foolishly and pathetically, doesn't.

We are encouraged into the position of a rapist in relation to her. For one thing, we can see her but she can't see us – this is true of all film and TV characters, obviously enough, but it is really played on here because it gets the female character into situations where, if she knew she could be seen, she'd be on her guard, she'd protect her body symbolically from our gaze with gestures and clothes. As it is however, the gothic heroine's nightgown is inadequately buttoned up so that her bosom glows in the candlelight; the escaping heroine who's caught her leg in something wriggles to get free and her skirt rides higher and higher up her thigh. Exposing the body makes flesh available to the gaze of whoever is around. Female flesh is thought to provoke the heterosexual male viewer; the sight of it can make him want to take it – the sight of it exposed by a woman in a vulnerable situation who is doubly vulnerable because she, as a character, doesn't know we're sitting there in the dark watching. This puts us in the classic rapist-watching-in-the-shadows position. Some-times, quite often in fact, we are even more explicitly put in the rapist's position. We see the heroine from the point of view of the lurking fiend, psychopath or monster. One of the commonest climactic camera shots in sequences like this has the heroine backing away from the camera, looking at it in terror, cringing in helplessness. She is looking at us; we are the raging fiend.

But she is rescued by the hero, who is our stand-in, our identification figure. The camera puts us in the position of the rapist, but the plot puts us reassuringly back in the position of the saviour. This once again establishes our superiority – she needed the man/us to come to her rescue, she'll now be in our debt, subordinate to our masterful actions. (If this is none too edifying for the male audience, heaven knows what it does for women in the audience.)

The stock-in-trade of popular film and television is the pleasure of thrills, terror and horror, and there is nothing inherently objectionable in this. What is at issue is the way these pleasures are time and time again set up for us in ways that equate the general excitement of suspense and tension with sexual excitement, power over women, the thrill of taking a woman and the reassurance of female subordination. In such sequences we are not so much shown men nor men's sexuality as invited to see and feel it. We are invited to place ourselves in relation to women as heterosexual men, easily and uncontrollably aroused by the sight of women, heady in power over the weak.

A second commonplace sequence also asks us to identify with heterosexual feelings, to agree with its idea of what heterosexual male feelings are; it also encourages us to go on believing such feelings exist. This sequence shows the moment when the hero first sees the heroine, when he looks at her with love or desire. It goes something like this: shot of hero looking at something off camera, he lit in standard lighting; long, held shot of heroine looking down or away, not at the hero, lit in soft glow, glamour lighting; back to shot of him looking at her. The conventions of matching shots make it absolutely clear that he is looking at her but she doesn't know that he is. Sometimes, towards the end of the shot she will look in his direction, but only momentarily; then she will avert her eyes. As Nancy Henley shows in her book *Body Politics*, this reproduces the convention of looks and glances in actual heterosexual exchanges. Men stare at women, women submit to being looked at, or at most steal a glance.

The fact that the woman often doesn't know she is being looked at once again makes her vulnerable. And, once again, we are invited to relate to the heroine through this version of heterosexual male sexuality. We don't see male arousal, the hero seldom speaks or expresses his feelings, there is no exploration of those feelings from the outside – all there is is an encouragement to experience male sexuality in the act of looking, looking at the screen, looking at women.

I've been describing two very commonplace sequences. Many have argued that the devices used, the way the camera places us as voyeur, the way editing puts us into the position of the male, the way the narrative encourages us to identify with the man, compose the very basic storytelling grammar of mainstream film and television fiction. The argument can be taken further to suggest that virtually all narratives, regardless of what medium they are in, reproduce the way male sexuality is organized, to the extent that it is hard to tell whether narrative structure is based on how we think of male sexuality or whether our conception of male sexuality is derived from the pleasures of male dominance within narratives.

There is a suggestive similarity in the way both male sexuality and narrative are commonly described. Male sexuality is said to be goal-orientated; seduction and foreplay are merely the means by which one gets to the 'real thing', an orgasm, the great single climax. Equally, it has been suggested that if one compares the underlying structure of most narratives in western fiction it is about the pursuit of a goal and its attainment, usually through possession. Thus male sexuality is like a story, or stories are like male sexuality. Both keep women in their place.

Since men are the central protagonists of all but a few specifically feminine narrative genres (for instance, romance), and are also the ones given the active roles as the characters who make things happen and who move the narrative along, women function either as the goal of the narrative or as the reward for achieving that goal. In this way, narratives reproduce the connection with sexuality. Even if the narrative appears to be about war, crime, business or whatever, the drive to a climax is so bound up with the promise of a woman at the end that all stories seem to be modelled on male sexuality. It is no accident that the word climax applies to orgasm and narrative. In both, the climax is at once what sex and story aim at; the climax is also the signal that the sex and the story are over. The placing of the women and the men in stories ensures that a heterosexual model is reasserted, in which women represent what male sexuality is ostensibly there for. Women are the goal or the reward, they are the occasion of male sexuality – and yet they play no active part in it. The man drives himself, or his penis drives him; it is he who 'reaches' the climax.

Are all narratives like this? Must they be? What I've described is an overall *tendency* in twentieth-century media fiction; it is economical, dynamic, efficient, finished – qualities we are brought up to respect and qualities which as *part of* the spectrum of human qualities, have much to commend them. But it is by no means only in elite and experimental fiction that we can find something else. The complex frustrations of *film noir* narrative, the unending multiple climaxes of soap opera, the way song numbers in most musicals interrupt narrative flow as expressions of mutual delight between people, the episodic structure of many comedies and some adventure stories, which dispense with the idea of a goal as such – all these suggest that there is room for manoeuvre, not only in terms of woman-centred narratives, but also in terms of stories centred around either sex that are not told and felt through the eyes of an oppressive male sexuality.

One would not and should not expect a society run in the interests of men to produce images that go against this. The visual representation of male sexuality puts women in their place, as objects of a 'natural' male sexual drive that may at times be ridiculous but is also insistent, inescapable and inevitable. Such representations help preserve the existing power relations of men over women by translating them into sexual relations, rendered both as biologically given and as a source of masculine pleasure. What is perhaps more surprising is that these images should, by and large, be so unattractive, so straight and narrow, so dreary. Men too are fixed in place by this imagery, and if theirs is a place of superiority it is nonetheless a cramped, sordid, compulsive little place with its hard-edged contours and one-off climaxes.

No society is unified and homogenous. If it were, change could not be imagined, there could be no images of something else. There are other images of male sexuality – in some gay and feminist art, which is where you'd hope to find it, and also within the mainstream, popular (but largely unrespectable) traditions of comedy and romance. Here and there we do get a vision of a sexuality that is not nasty and brutish, silly and pathetic, but varied, sensuous, langorous, warm and welcome. We need to see it more often in order to live it more fully.

4. Pornography

Pornography is now big business. According to one estimate the pornography industry in the USA – encompassing the output of videos, films, books, magazines and 'sex aids' – had a turnover equal to that of the conventional film and music industries combined – some four billion dollars in 1977. It is also a very profitable business. A market analysis estimates that an enterprising entrepreneur need only invest $3,500 in setting up an 'adult' bookshop in a good location, in return for which he could expect a profit of $50,000 after one year.[1] Given this licence to print money it is not surprising that in America, at least, the pornography industry has been one of the fastest growth sectors in the economy over the last decade. Although the scale of operations in Britain is not so large, the proliferation of pornographic bookshops testifies to a similar dynamic here. This has caused a degree of pious alarm in official British circles with measures discussed or introduced which include: the licensing of pornographic bookshops; the outlawing of child pornography; and the crackdown on gay pornography.

This enormous growth has gone hand in hand with an expansion of pornography for heterosexual men into the respectable market place. The multitude of pornographic magazines available in newsagents, even on the shelves of the biggest operators like W. H. Smiths, makes pornography available well beyond the confines of the 'dirty' bookshop to a mass market of men. This expansion has brought with it the location of several pornography markets roughly corresponding to the division between hard and soft core pornography. Specialist retailers in pornography now confine their attentions to the lucrative trade in hard core pornography, arbitrarily regulated by the law and the interventions of the police and customs officials.

As the hard core stuff has come out from under the counter, soft pornography has moved out of the sex shops altogether and into the mainstream retail market. This shift has become well established, to the point where the physical presence of soft pornography is taken for granted; its imagery informs the contents of a range of media beyond what is normally classified as pornography. Men's leisure interest magazines in particular – *Amateur Photographer* for example – include images which wouldn't be out of place in *Playboy* or *Mayfair*. More ambiguously the imagery of some magazines for women, for instance *Cosmopolitan*, and advertising campaigns aimed at both women and men, share a language of display of women and women's bodies similar to that used in soft pornography.[2] The distinction between hard and soft core pornography is not fixed and definite; what is now considered acceptable in soft pornography would have been classified as hard pornography less than 20 years ago. The interacting legal and commercial considerations of obscenity and acceptability have helped shape these distinctions through time.

Pornography – hard or soft core – depicts women as limited beings with a restricted sexual presence subservient to apparently specific masculine desires. The distinction between the two 'genres' is a matter of degree and specialist codification, with hard core pornography closing down the range of representations in image or text to narrow specialities, fragmenting the female body into minute classifications (large breasts, large bums, vaginas), or dressing the whole body according to the codes of fetishisms, such as sado-masochism. Alongside these forms are those which include men enacting codified desires upon women – fucking them, humiliating them, inflicting mock or, at the extreme, real violence upon them.

These forms of pornography are, on the face of it, light years away from the tasteful soft focus of the likes of

Penthouse magazine, but I would argue that the 'hardest' or most extreme variants of pornography share with the most accessible soft pornography a distinct structuring of men's desires; the imagery of the woman in pornography is the doubly alienated embodiment of and for these desires. To this end, I want to analyse the structure of meanings contained within soft pornography given the cultural predominance it has established, and partly also because I know the genre, having used it for fantasizing with and masturbating in preference to the more obviously desperate and depressing specialities provided by hard core pornography. I have also chosen to look at magazines – specifically *Playboy*, *Mayfair* and *Knave* – in preference to other forms of pornography available. These three magazines cover a range of form and content within soft pornography, from the oldest and best established one, *Playboy*, which has become synonymous with the genre, to the more explicitly pornographic *Knave*, at the boundary of soft and hard core. In analysing these magazines I want to explore the relationship men have to (soft) pornography: how does it work as a sexual turn on? What does it say about our sexuality? (And what does it *not* say?) What does it say about what it is to be a man in a general social sense?

These are the kind of questions that men have hardly started to ask as far as I know,[3] even though the whole matter of pornography has been a major issue for feminists since the late 1970s, an issue fuelled by the anger women have felt when confronted by the steady increase in pornographic output. In questioning the 'truth' about women that pornography articulates – that women crave the phallic desire of men, that this is their essence, that this is what they really want – feminists have issued a challenge to the complicity between men and pornography. However, the emphasis of this challenge, which has set the agenda for the feminist debate on pornography, has tended to underscore the conservative assumption that masculine sexuality and identity is natural and pre-given, and that pornography expresses the truth about men. Thus the growth of violent pornography as a sub-stream of pornography has been identified by writers such as Andrea Dworkin[4] as reflecting the essential violence of masculine sexuality. Following from this, the explosion of pornography into the mass market place is explained as an aggressive assertion of phallic power and an incitement to men to act this out, violently if necessary, on women's bodies. The 'truth' about men's sexuality, formerly covert and illicit, is now boldly trumpeted across the land.

At its bleakest, this position offers no hope for change, and worst of all confirms the stereotypes of aggressive masculinity acting upon passive femininity, with men as victors and women as victims. I offer what follows as a challenge to this assumption and the silence that surrounds it.

Order and chaos

The understandings men have about our sexuality are determined by the more general meanings available to us as to what it is to be a man. When asked by Shere Hite what qualities make 'a man a man', men replied with a list of characteristics that situated sex low down on the hierarchy of priorities. Most important was that a man should be 'self-assured, unafraid, in control and autonomous, or self-sufficient, not dependent'. Other qualities, such as leadership, the ability to 'take charge', and dependability were given as variations on this central theme.[5] Whether many men actually experience *themselves* as having such qualities is doubtful, but it is important to recognize that these qualities are what men expect (and fear) in each other as well as expect of themselves.

The problem with this, of course, is that men can only sustain this public sense of themselves in a world where we expect and demand that women cater to our needs, materially and emotionally, in exchange for the income and social status that we provide. Unable to look after ourselves, we carry our dependence from mother to lover or wife, concealed behind this unequal exchange. Women have always recognized this dependency but have been expected to keep it to themselves.

Since the 1950s however, social and economic shifts have occurred that have weakened the structure of men's dominance of the public world, and that have provided new ground for women to question their complicity with men and to withdraw it on a scale not socially possible 25 years ago. The former certainties that a woman should 'love, honour and obey' her husband in marriage structured women's complicity with men's dominance and provided the grounds for enforcing it if necessary; these structures no longer retain their authority. The circumstances and nature of women's complicity, formerly rendered unproblematic and invisible for men, are no longer so secure and unproblematic. This has had a profound and disorientating impact upon the traditional authority of masculine identity, an impact which men have sought to resist in new ways. Pornography's place in relation to these changed circumstances is important, I believe, for two reasons. Firstly soft pornography proposes that women's complicity with men's predominance is taken for granted and therefore secure, and secondly it provides a focus for the assertion of male dominance in the world. By doing so, pornography can serve to conjure up for us as men a concrete sense of ourselves, a sense which can otherwise be more illusory than the glossy pages of pornography itself.

One of the reasons male identity is now so unstable arises from the fact that men are no longer so likely to be the household's sole breadwinner. In the last 25 years women have entered the workforce in increasing numbers. Although restricted to the lowest paid jobs in the main, many women now earn an income in their own right, necessary for the maintenance of the household. There has, however, been no commensurate shift in the domestic division of labour. Women now face working a double shift, with responsibilities for home and children as well as paid employment.[6] The added pressure that this has placed on women has put a tremendous strain on their collusion in bolstering men's domestic and emotional helplessness. The traditional strategies that men have used to avoid housework and child care – 'work to do which comes first, meetings to go to, buddies to meet in the pub' – are wearing thin.[7] As women have become earners in their own right so men have less social and economic power to trade in return for emotional 'understanding' and support. Consequently men's emotional insecurity and dependency have become more apparent and acute.

Sexuality has had a significant role in articulating these tensions as the strains of domestic conflict have combined with tensions in the expression of sexual desire itself. This is particularly painful because of the emotional force bound up with sexual desire and because sex is the one part of our lives that we expect to be free from the pressures of the daily round. As Tony Eardley put it:

> One of the most abiding and seductive myths that all of us, men and women, are instilled with from our first understandings of love and sex is that the bed, the privacy of 'freely' exchanged sexual love is that one place where we cast off the world with our clothes and become anonymous, essential, lost in oneness with our partner.[8]

This expectation has, if anything, been heightened by the volume of press advice, encouragement and instruction on better, more satisfying, sexual experience. However, as we are assured of the normality and naturalness of this wonderful enterprise, the conscious care and attention given to defining precisely what is good, normal and natural testifies to the increasingly problematic nature of sexuality. At a basic level the 'problematic' is women's exploration of their sexuality; as we shall see with pornography, the 'narrative of the (female) orgasm has become the staple fare of sexology'.[9] Of men's sexuality however relatively little has been written. Men writing fiction dealing with the sexuality of men represent male sexuality in a mythical and unsatisfactory way. This may well be because 'their own sexuality arouses too much anxiety to be successfully represented'.[10]

Historically this anxiety has been concealed within a tradition that places men's sexuality in the realm of biology, a matter of natural urges, of which the female of the species is the natural object. Within this tradition a man is driven by his desire to take and penetrate a woman. His erection is the centrepiece for the sexual encounter; it is the organizing principle. All other bodily faculties and possibilities are secondary to this one. A woman's vagina exists to be penetrated, the penis-erect to penetrate. This is the essence of phallocentrism. I would venture that few men, if any, experience themselves or women in this way. But no matter how actual experience spills over this narrow regime of sexual practice it remains, like the more general structure of masculinity, a powerful organizing force.

As women challenge this regime, sexuality has become increasingly problematic for men. The anxieties induced by unreal standards – not being able to 'get' an erection at the appropriate time, 'prematurely' ejaculating, and the more general sense of having to be ready for sex no matter what the immediate circumstances or feelings – are gradually being forced to the surface. These are all anxieties attendant on the performance principle.

Alongside this self-conscious sense of having to 'do it right' men invest phallic sexuality with an emotional force that borders on the romantic. Shere Hite reports, to her obvious surprise, that most men in her survey liked and wanted intercourse for the emotional warmth and tenderness it allowed them to express, and for the feeling of being loved and accepted. The possibility of freely expressing and receiving love and affection however is attenuated by the mannerisms of phallic desire and the subtle or not so subtle pressures attendant on it. Sexuality focuses the need to be loved and accepted as a person who is more than the sum of his public (controlling and authoritative) attributes. But as these elements of masculinity remain predominant, vulnerability and dependence can easily become intensely threatening and isolating emotions, magnified by the fear of being 'found out'. In these circumstances it is not surprising that men's sexual desire often appears to women as an obdurate force of unstated or codified needs.

In a careful and perceptive analysis drawn from her own and her friends' experience, Wendy Hollway identifies the ambiguity that men express about their sexual feelings towards women as a response to the vulnerability that this brings with it. 'Intense feelings of involvement and need, the danger to one's separate identity, wanting to have somebody forever and fearing that they will let you down' are feelings which are threatening to men precisely because they cannot be easily admitted, if at all.[11] They run counter to men's equally strong need to be invulnerable and distant. Thus one man Hollway interviewed expressed a fear of being 'sucked into' a relationship with a woman as a consequence of a sexual encounter. In other words we translate *our* fear for ourselves into a fear of *their* dependency and vulnerability.

Men therefore expect women to provide them with sexual and emotional security, but women are in turn feared for having a powerful insight into men's insecurity. As Hollway argues, gender inequality has traditionally allowed men to exsternalize these tensions by projecting them onto women.

> [Women] have already been constructed in such a way that they manifest the [emotional] characteristics that men are suppressing. Likewise [women] experience themselves as wanting commitment and, materially, are more likely to be in a position of needing it, because this is how they have been positioned historically.[12]

The contradictions inherent in masculine authority have been traditionally sustained in this way, with women as the 'natural' bearers of the nurturing, comforting role bringing understanding and support to the knotted tensions and insecurities lying beneath the surface of men's public persona. As women have remained isolated in the home, so these masculine tensions have remained hidden, private, as sacred and vulnerable as men's 'private parts'. The time-honoured strategies that men have used to distance themselves from this underlying insecurity are themselves predicated upon the security of the private domain and the silence or unintelligibility of women's 'nagging' or 'gossip'.

Confronted with the economic, social, political and sexual shifts in relationships with women, men can no longer rely unquestioningly on the security of the private realm. One indicator of the resulting tensions is the statistical probability that one marriage in three is likely to end in divorce; women sue for the great majority of divorces (8 out of 10).[13] Related to this, questions of wage and job equality, domestic and child care responsibilities, sexuality, and emotionality are now on a *public* agenda, put there by the women's movement. Men's traditional strategies of evasion in these circumstances are less credible because increasingly transparent.

The rise of mass market pornography is, I believe, a consequence of these personal and social struggles. It provides a vicarious means of escape and solace for men. It displays the old assumptions of women's subordination and their complicity in it, in the teeth of all the changes to the contrary.

Private pleasures

Pornography asserts itself as a domain separate from the everyday world, or as a window on to a realm of the purely sexual. Within this world all women are universalized to become 'woman'; her essential being is laid bare as sexual. By extension, this world situates all men as 'man' with the essentially phallic being expressed in his sexuality. The male reader is thus welcomed as a member of the brotherhood of all men, united with them in the fact of his gaze and the 'itch in his groin'.[14] The power of this message lies in the emphasis upon the attributes of controlled and authoritative masculinity that are common currency, and the apparent exclusion of all fears and anxieties attendant upon this principle. Pornography's message therefore provides reassurance: the man who buys the magazine is confirmed in his masculinity; he is normal, healthy and in control.

If we stand back from this we find ourselves faced with a massive conceit. Although pornography asserts virile sexuality, it is not about 'real sex' with women; it is a carefully constructed substitute. And yet, in such a careful construction lies the message that this separate domain is nothing more than the essential quality of masculinity that the reader desires. The gap between this promise and the reader's own experience acts as an incitement to him to forget himself and become a 'real man', essential, unified with other men by lust for all desirable women.

Men read and gaze at the contents of soft core pornographic magazines to engage in sexual fantasy by themselves. In consequence of course, masturbation and not sexual intercourse with a woman is the natural counterpart to pornography.

As Angela Carter suggests:

> An increase of pornography on the market, within the purchasing capacity of the common man . . . does not mean an increase in sexual licence . . . It might only indicate a more liberal attitude to masturbation, rather than to fucking, and reinforces a solipsistic concentration on the relationship with the self, which is a fantasy one at the best of times.[15]

While masturbating, a man can control his own sexual pleasure unaffected by performance anxiety or by the sexual desire of a partner. He can lay aside the emotional and material conflicts which impinge on a sexual relationship and concentrate upon his own desire. Pornographic magazines make available numerous images and texts of sexual meaning for men, which are available as source material for fantasy. No man can absorb or consume all these meanings, but that's not the point. What is significant is that he is being offered material over which he can exercise a superficial degree of choice and control, expressed in preferences for this or that model, this or that gesture, and so on. Pornography provides an order for sexual fantasy which affirms the orderliness of phallocentrism, sexual fantasy which can be acted out on the instrument of that order, the erection.

Richard Wollheim has expressed this relationship thus:

> The work (of pornography) can be seen as igniting our sexuality, or as dominating it and making it move to a strict tempo; or as inundating it with confused possibilities; or as preserving it from contact with other feelings ... or as trivializing it, aggrandizing it, degrading it, *but always ruthlessly controlling it*. [my emphasis][16]

Woman's body

When a man buys a pornographic magazine, the main thing he looks for is pictorial display of nude women. The text of the magazines, the articles, cartoons, jokes and advertisements seem, at first sight, to be a relatively indistinct background, filling in the space between the pictures.

The relationship of the male reader to these images has several interlinked layers of meaning. At a primary level the almost universal use of colour photography conjures up a powerful sense of realism projecting each woman's presence and availability. In a different context John Berger wrote:

> [Colour] photography can reproduce the colour and texture and tangibility of objects as only oil paint had been able to do before. Colour photography is to the spectator-buyer what oil paint is to the spectator-owner. Both media use similar highly tactile means to play upon the spectator's sense of acquiring the *real* thing which the image shows. In both cases his feelings that he can almost touch what is in the image reminds him how he might or does possess the real thing.[17]

There are certain conventions that pornography requires its women models to adopt in their poses and gestures, the most significant of these being the gaze directed to return the reader's gaze. This gaze emphasizes the woman's presence in a manner which is personalized and colludes with the reader's intent. It establishes the ground upon which the male reader can enact his sexual desire in fantasy, by positing him as sexually desirable. With relief the reader can mingle his fantasies of desire with the images of the woman offering herself to him.

The complicity of the woman runs through all the images available to the reader, because it is so crucial to the workings of pornography. To work, it must establish a universe in which all men are sexually desirable, because they are desired. All women are just dying to be taken by you, the reader. It works by denying the reality which men know and often fear to be true. Sex is not unproblematic but is beset by complications and anxieties – those of sexual isolation, clumsiness, 'inadequacy', the tension attendant on 'doing it right', of not being or feeling sexually desirable. It is in the space between this anxiety and the fantasy realm of a perfect sexual world that pornography achieves its power, offering the reader the promise that he is desirable, with sexual metaphors – the images of women – of and for his own desire.

The growing 'explicitness' of representation is a manifestation of this tension. Many images within soft core pornography now focus on women's genitals in a way that would have been labelled 'hard core' only a few years ago. Even the most widely available magazines like *Playboy* have felt impelled to include a growing number of such images. Two styles predominate. In the first the model is looking directly at the reader. In many such images she is reclining on a bed or a couch. The 'look' of complicity is underpinned by the sight of her genitals. This exposure offers her sex to the reader as a vagina offered for his erection to penetrate. His desire is established as pre-eminent, hers is neutralized. The second style is markedly different. It depicts a woman rapt in sexual ecstasy. Her eyes are closed, her body arched with orgasmic tension. In many images her fingers touch her clitoris, as though she is masturbating. Her pleasure is self-expressed, but she remains firmly within the male gaze.

At least two interpretations of this type of image are possible. It almost always appears as part of a sequence which includes more 'traditional' poses of the 'returning-the-gaze-of-the-reader' variety. As the 'climax' of a sequence it articulates the rapture of penetration, fulfilled in her orgasm; the efficacy of the reader's erection is confirmed. Another meaning which may exist alongside the first without contradicting it, lies in the simple fact of the complete exposure of her genitals to the male gaze. The woman's sexual desire, the siting of her sexual pleasure in her clitoris is focused on in order to 'demystify' this terrifying fact, by crystallizing it and alienating it from her in the possessed image. The two meanings interplay, in fact to neutralize and marginalize the sexuality of the woman and to reassert the pre-eminence and normality of penetration.

This closing in of the male gaze is a response to the growing fact of women's sexual independence and the mixture of acute anxiety and fascination which this has induced in men able to cope only with the fantasy of women's passive sexuality. A woman's desire for her own orgasm is transmuted into a clinical representation of the flesh of her sexual organs. It is as if, by staring hard enough, the reader can somehow come to possess and master her subversive sexual difference.

These tensions are dealt with more explicitly in the texts of pornographic magazines. Letters telling of sexual adventures and exploits (probably all fictional), phoney 'scientific' sexological studies of sexual behaviour and explicitly fictional pieces, even the blurb accompanying adverts for sexual aids articulate the heroic tale of the erection and its mission to penetrate women's vaginas.

Within these fictions women's desire is centred on wanting, if not craving to be penetrated by the male protagonist. 'I found myself getting excited, aching to be filled' says the woman in one short story. 'She shuddered and moaned with delight as I kissed her wet crack, [until] she was really asking for it' boasts the man in another tale. The moment of penetration and the rhythms of fucking rise up and down on the page until the climactic moment of the man and the woman's orgasm is reached in wonderful unison. 'Feeling me coming sent her over the top as well and she screamed as she came.' 'It was delirium when he came – it made me all gooey, a sort of blackout.' What these fictions assert is that a woman's sexual pleasure is attendant upon the penetration and rhythms of the erection. More than this, the woman's orgasm expresses a delight in the fact of male sexual fulfilment. As he comes so does she. The fact that this assertion was counter to most women's experience can only suggest the depth of anxiety and confusion among men which this standardized scenario addresses.

The expression of a woman's delight so lovingly detailed in these fictions points to a further and very profound source of despair amongst men. Without exception the descriptions of the 'foreplay' and the act itself is articulated in two parts. The man does things to the woman, the woman enjoys what he is doing to her. Take this for instance:

> Inch by inch I started to kiss every part of her body; she was whimpering and panting by the end of this, and I knew I was in for a good lay. So I positioned myself, and without warning, gave a giant first thrust right into her fanny. She yelled with excitement so much that I rammed nearly as hard the second time. Then I slowed my pace, and pumped at her more gently, keeping up a good rhythm. I soon quickened as I felt her quivering. Then with a giant final thrust I pushed right into her, and felt her muscles clench hard around me as I spurted inside her. She yelled as she climaxed, her head wagging from side to side.

The man depicted here might as well not have a body. He is nothing more than the rhythms of his erection. He expresses no pleasure or joy in 'the act'. He is silent as he concentrates on the job. She by contrast lies back and takes what he thrusts upon her. She loves it, of course. Her moans and yells testify to the efficacy of his cock, and yet she expresses a sexual pleasure which he does not. His automaton-like ejaculation triggers orgasm in the woman. He on the other hand articulates no pleasure or orgasm in this moment; it simply happens. He is silent.

Through pornography woman's body is the site of sexual pleasure for the male reader, determined by his gaze, the model's posture, and the fictional act of penetration. It is a pleasure consequent upon the male act, but not shared by the actor himself – either as reader or as fictional sexual hero. This alienation from pleasure is interwoven with an envy of the pleasure pornography allows women to express. This is apparent in the fake orgasm images discussed before. While the man reading and looking at pornography is assured that he is desirable, the object-woman that desires him betokens magical sexual powers and pleasures which are alien to him. The reader's cock becomes the object of a desire offered to him as his own, but without the substance to ever be anything other than an illusion.

Ultimately then, the subordination of women to the thrusts of masculine sexuality doesn't pay off, even within the pages of pornography. Men might set the rules, but women are shown to come out enjoying it most. The gap never closes between the magic attempt to possess pleasure in the body of a woman and the continual elusiveness of that pleasure, even while possessing an erection. The whole circular process just spins on and on under its own momentum. Being 'in control' of phallic desire allows men the possession of the means of their own alienation; the pornographers are on hand to sell us the message that this is what we most desire.

Sexual casualties

It is no coincidence that the pornographic magazines which strain hardest to celebrate the normality of this sexual universe should contain echoes of sexual anxieties, fears and 'inadequacies' in their sexual scenarios and in the small print of adverts for sex aids. In this sense the pornographic fiction has a second meaning to that already discussed. Alongside women's craving for penetration lies the counterpart of men's need to satisfy this lust. From being in complicity with phallic desire, and in celebration of it – 'Yes! Yes! Screw me!' – women's desire for penetration becomes a demand which has to be met. Thus the abundance of *choice* presented to satisfy phallic desire becomes, within the pornographic scenario, an onus upon the man to satisfy the limitless *demands* placed before him. Not surprisingly this is a pretty gruelling regime, and like all regimes it has its own precise set of rules and regulations and severe penalties for those who err.

First, there is penis size. 'Ronnie has a four-inch cock and a long foreskin. When erect, it measures just over six inches, and five inches around.' For comparison, we are told of two unnamed twin brothers who 'both have identically-sized cocks – exactly eight and a half inches'. The message is: the bigger the better: quantity equals quality. Without the proper equipment you might as well not bother. With penises properly sized, checked and in order we next pass on to the matter or sexual technique. Firstly, *get* an erection. 'His penis was sticking out of his flies and was obviously ready for action.' This sets the correct tone for the sexual encounter. It shows that the man is alert, and in command of the situation. 'Foreplay', including varieties of oral sex, is to be encouraged as a prelude to fucking. Women like oral sex and this can provide a man with new opportunities to display his mastery of technique. As 'Carol' reports from Yorkshire, her husband 'loves to get his head between my thighs and when he tongues my clit I just keep on coming'. Furthermore, too brusque an approach to fucking may well be off-putting for some women, and besides, being sucked off yourself can be very enjoyable. Finally, the fuck itself. Any position is okay, although the more adventurous postures are commended. Remember, not too fast. Listen to what 'Jane' has to say on the subject of Ronnie's technique; 'He's not one to ram it up me and fuck like mad until he comes. He likes to make it last, shagging me slowly, sometimes long, deep, slow strokes, sometimes, short, fast ones. Stopping so he can "cool down" and then starting again, getting me to the point where I MUST come.' Ronnie is an example to us all with his excellent technique bringing out the best in Jane. Very good Ronnie – and lucky Jane.

Correct equipment and technique are, then, the necessary essentials that a man needs for sexual success. However, these elements are not enough in themselves without the proper motivation, the proper drive, the will to make it happen. In fact lack of the will to do it probably means that the man has not got the basic equipment either. The penalty for this failing will be desertion by wife or girlfriend when the man has not got the proper phallic power.

> My second husband and I have been married for three years and we enjoy fucking anywhere and everywhere. My first husband said I was a nymphomaniac, but now I realize that I am normal and it is he who has the problem. I wanted sex more frequently than he would or could provide. This led to rows and subsequent divorce. The real reason for the divorce was Martin, my new husband. He was always ready with a stiff prick.

Moreover, *looking* like a real man is no good in itself without the will to have sex as this sorry tale of Rose's 'frustration' testifies:

> She thought briefly of the nights she had lain beside Alan, anxious for his attention, yet always unsatisfied. She remembered how she had longed for sexual con-summation and how she felt ashamed when her friends had quizzed her about her supposedly virile Adonis husband.

These scenarios are like short morality plays or fables on the subject (and object) of phallic desire and power. The basic moral of all of them is that having phallic power is essential to being a man. Now this is problematic in itself. If this essential 'manly' quality is a natural state of masculinity, why is it so necessary to conduct such careful examinations of behaviour to judge it correct and laudable or incorrect and therefore contemptible? This tension between normalcy and deviance, the good and the bad, gives these discourses a ruthless double edge. In one moment frailties are touched on – the embarrassment of an attempted seduction, the fear of ageing – only to be swept reassuringly away as the man in question realises his phallic potential and consummates his sexuality and his masculine being to the applause of his partner's ecstatic cries. There is a 'phew, made it' quality to these stories. 'Try harder' is a message to those who fear their phallic potential slipping away. Not to want to try, not to want to 'do it' is the worst sin of all. In the realm of almost tangible sexual anxiety and paranoia these fables have a clear and contemptuous meaning for those seen to fail: 'You're not a man, you're nothing.'

The most pernicious aspect of all this is the use of women as narrators of the tales. In one and the same breath this establishes the normalcy and naturalness of the whole enterprise and places the burden of the control or policing of sex on the prized but alien objects of phallic heroism. If a man hasn't got what it takes to be a man it will be a woman who will know, a woman who will reject him in favour of a man who has. In the last analysis women are responsible and women are to blame.

Phallic plastic

Phallic power is an unrelenting treadmill which threatens to collapse at any moment under the weight of its contradictions; woe betide the man who stumbles. The constant awareness of such a possibility informs the fictions of pornography with a manic, unyielding quality.

Needless to say, the burden this places on men is immense. In examining the male pin-up Richard Dyer identifies the instabilities inherent in phallic masculinity as they appear framed in these images. The crucial weakness lies with the image of the penis.

> The fact is the penis isn't a patch on the phallus. The penis can never live up to the mystique implied by the phallus. Hence the excessive, even hysterical quality of so much male imagery. The clenched fists, the bulging muscles, the hardened jaws . . . are all straining after what can hardly ever be achieved, the embodiment of the phallic mystique.[18]

For this straining for the unachievable has its counterpart in pornographic fiction: an obsession with quantities. The size of the penis (limp or erect), the number of times a man fucks, the number of different postures he initiates, the scale and quantity of the orgasms he brings his partner to; all these show a desperation to attain and sustain phallic identity in the face of near impossible odds. The whole regime is absurd, of course, but the anxieties that stem from it are felt deeply and commonly enough by men to keep a small industry producing quack products at inflated prices to provide the 'inadequate' with renewed and invigorated phallic potential.

Adverts for 'sexual aids' make depressing reading. For those unable to maintain an erection, Dr Blakoe's 'Energizer Ring' promises that this is a simple and effective way for men to regain their potency. 'Improved performance results have been published in leading Medical Journals.' For example:

> One [doctor's] patient was a fit and active 60-year-old who found that after wearing the Blakoe Energizer Ring (around the base of his penis) for only three weeks, his erections had become 40 to 50 per cent more rigid and his frequency of intercourse had increased from three or four per month to eight per month. There was also a definite increase in muscle tone and penile dimension.

For those men who are traumatized by the belief that their penises are too small the same company offers free a 'Penis Vacuum Developer' – available in three sizes, 'for aiding Penile Enlargement and preventing shrinkage of the Penis'.

Sprays, creams and ointments are offered to help maintain the erection or to help avoid 'premature ejaculation'. Tablets, pills and exotic-sounding herbs promise to 'increase your sexual urge' or to provide the reader with 'a little extra energy for those wonderful "Marathon Sessions" you love so much'.

These sales blurbs make one thing perfectly clear: phallic desire is a matter of alienated work, the instrument of that work being the male body, or more precisely the erection. As desire within this realm is reified to become a matter of efficient equipment, production techniques, and output quotas, so the remedies made available for a sexual problem address it as one of mechanical dysfunction, much like a car with a faulty starter-motor. If necessary, 'serious' medical evidence can be wheeled on to provide a rational scientific legitimacy for the manufacturer's product. Rather than explain anything, however, this device serves only to underscore the irrational, object-world of phallic desire, and poses a number of important questions about the role of science as an ideology.

The alienation from sexual desire and pleasure that these adverts articulate represents a depth of sexual bewilderment that can be described as an autism – a self enclosed fantasy world of sexual mystification conducted to the rhythm of the phallic regime. What other sense can be made of a desperation as profound and confused as that represented in adverts for 'getting girls' by means of hypnosis, or for scent containing 'the undetectable female attractant pheromone which attracts women without them being aware of it.' This is the netherworld of phallic failure; as pornography beats out the tempo of what it takes to be a man so it offers the solace of ointments, pills and plastic equipment to the defeated and the frightened – at the right price, you understand.

The circle is finally closed with the adverts for dildos and plastic vagina. 'Triple Ripple – just plug this three-ridged dildo into your woman and give her the feeling of being opened up to you as never before!' Or, 'Big Brother – Give her ten inches of thick, vibrating penetration and she'll never know what hit her. Show her what a deep orgasm feels like and watch her love it!' Or, if you can't get it up yourself, use a plastic substitute on her. The alienation from sexual desire is complete; phallic power finally collapses into the fantasy inherent within it. And then, if you haven't got a woman, why not use 'the Constant Power Ejaculator, the perfect masturbation device. It plugs in and can stroke, vibrate, and actually feel as good as the real thing, without having to beg!'

Misogyny and men's rage

The logic of phallic desire is squarely grounded upon the subordination of women's sexual desire. Sexual intimacy, the expression of sexual pleasure, or fun or joy, is constrained by this order to the point where men have no language of sexual expression except that articulated by proxy through women. A woman's moans of pleasure in pornographic fiction articulate both the efficacy of the thrusting penis and the alienation of sexual enjoyment from phallic practice. The sexual oppression of women organized and articulated within the pages of pornography represents in part the need men have to capture sexual pleasure in a woman's body, from which they are alienated. The siting of sexuality in a woman's body is thus a source of great yearning, and also a source of frustration and rage. Women keep the secret, the secret of bodily pleasure, to themselves and from men, who strain long and hard for it; for this, women are envied and resented. This idea is implicit in the phallic myths sold by the tests and images of mainstream pornography. Explicit misogyny erupts in the sex and sales hype or in cartoons and jokes. Many of these target women as objects of contempt and ridicule – the dumb blonde who's only good for one thing, or whose body is an incitement to penetration but who is romantic and sexually 'naive'; the woman who is unattractive, old or ugly, the feminist woman; the lesbian woman, and the pregnant woman. These targets represent the fearful world outside the neat boundaries evoked by pornography, a world peopled by women who are not all young and large-breasted and waiting quietly in the nude to give a man 'what he wants most'.

Playboy's middle age

Of the three magazines that I used for this research two, *Mayfair* and *Knave,* have dominated this discussion so far, particularly in relation to 'sexual casualties'. *Playboy* is noticeably different to most, if not all, other mass market soft core porno magazines. It is far more up-market, far glossier, far less explicitly pornographic than its competitors. It contains no pornographic fiction of the type I have discussed. It contains no advertising for sex aids. It does, of course, contain pornographic images of women and in this sense it shares with other magazines all the basic ideas of phallic orderliness I have looked at. Indeed, the *Playboy* centrefold and the 'Playmate of the Month' set the agenda for display which all other soft core porn magazines have followed. But it is the differences that are more interesting than the similarities.

Barbara Ehrenreich has analysed *Playboy*'s phenomenal growth in popularity in the 1950s and early 1960s as a challenge to the social imperative of the period that the middle-class male could only be a man if he was a husband and father and had a good job to provide for home and family.[19] The emphasis of this order was on 'mature responsibility'. *Playboy* said to hell with that – men should have fun. Not of the huntin', shootin', fishin' variety, which it ridiculed, but in the style of the sophisticated bachelor to which *Playboy*'s publisher, Hugh Hefner, himself aspired. The necessary accompaniment to this life style was the Playmate, the young, sexually available woman whom the aspiring executive would work with or meet socially out of hours. This was a scenario that definitely excluded marriage or breadwinning responsibilities; it also protected bachelors from the charge that it was tantamount to homosexuality to live on your own and read books.

By contrast, today *Playboy* has assumed the mantle of the mature heavyweight amongst 'men's magazines'. This is somewhat double-edged, as its falling circulation figures testify. The radical space it once occupied has now been usurped by magazines like *Mayfair* and *Knave*, which concentrate explicitly on pornography and have dispensed with interviews with Henry Kissinger. Uncertainties are now creeping in as others have overtaken *Playboy* in the process it initiated. Jokes now dwell on such formerly taboo subjects as homosexuality, and the risible fallibility of male heterosexual performance. Cartoons, which could be straight out of *The New Yorker* depict confused and embattled men dealing rather badly with exasperated wives and girlfriends. 'Little Debbie is pregnant by her uncle, Melanie has herpes, poor blind Bianca was raped by her tutor and you come home with a hard-on!' declaims an angry wife to her round-shouldered and pleading husband. I don't want to exaggerate this tendency – the uncertainties are very marginal to *Playboy* as a whole – but it reflects the middle age of a magazine and its readership caught between the faded fantasies of its youth and the brash cock-sure pornography of the younger generation.

What is also evident is that *Playboy*'s life style image reflects an age and class of readership with the economic means to realize the image on offer through consumption; sex is a crucial part of this, but only a part. It is very much the stuff of the American dream which never really survived the 1960s and Vietnam; no place here for sex aids or lurid sex stories. By contrast, the newer magazines reflect a far greater urgency and insecurity. The focus is on sex to the exclusion of practically all else. There is no life style attendant upon it either. As the explicitly pornographic content increases, so the adverts for expensive liquor and fast cars decrease, to be replaced by adverts for sex aids and cures for impotence. This reflects the lower-middle class and working-class readership to which the magazines are targeted; men who do not have the kind of income necessary to acquire the accoutrements of corporate masculinity and for whom sex is the locus of claustrophobic and pressing insecurities.

Conclusion

All soft pornography works by proposing that the reader is desirable because he is 'desired' by the women on display. A theme of complicity is established which unifies the desires of women and men around a phallocentric regime, implicit in the conventions of the images and explicit in the texts. This assertion of a predominant desire structures all the pornographic content and simultaneously provides a secure and 'legitimate' arena for the reader's fantasy. Every other theme in soft pornography derives from this one.

The images are key elements in providing this scenario. They focus, literally, on women alone, establishing their availability, their desire to be 'completed' by the reader: 'I'm here, I'm yours, take me.' The power of these images also derives from what Beverly Brown[20] called their 'everyday' quality. Situated in conventional interiors, or conventionally 'exotic' exteriors, the images exude an ordinariness, a quality which the caption writers seek to emphasize with reference to the model's personality, ambitions and so on. This quality is significant because women are ordinarily subjected to objectifying gender definitions of erotic or sexual status in the 'everyday' world. Soft pornography works then partly by re-emphasizing the ordinary quality of women's sexual objectification.

Looked at the other way round, this serves to confirm for the reader the 'everyday' assumptions regarding the power of his sexuality and its desirability. He can then place himself in the aura of desire projected by the woman, and become desirable himself. The tensions inherent in the phallic regime *externalize* a man's desire and reduce him to a silent shadow, a presence manifesting attributes of control and authority. This alienation from sexual desire is a problem taken up by the texts of soft pornography, in which the narratives of sex clearly distinguish between a physically active role for the man and a correspondingly passive role for the woman. However, as these narratives unfold it is clear that the man has a curiously *passive* role, without apparent motivation or desire beyond expressing the limited crudities which symbolize the social and physical force of his sexual predominance – 'I gave a giant first thrust right into her fanny.' Without exception, the woman is active in the sense that she is motivated by desire, albeit the desire to be taken and dominated, a desire which is invariably fulfilled with much orgasmic ecstasy.

Soft pornography works, then, by reasserting everyday assumptions about men's sexual predominance and women's subservience to that order. However, the actual mechanics of this order ascribe to women crucial sexual powers that men lack and need in equal measure. The tensions that this creates are presented in soft pornography in such a way as to make them safe and manageable for the reader. For example, the emphasis placed in pornographic narratives upon sexual performance, on doing a job properly, establishes a site of resistance to women's sexual desire by structuring it in such a way that a woman's sexual pleasure appears entirely dependent upon the determined expression of a man's sexual authority.

At the same time, however, pornography cannot *resolve* this tension – how could it? Instead, alongside the glowing colour renditions of women gazing expectantly at the reader, the cartoons, jokes and small ads express a contempt and fear of women that is the natural counterpart to their exalted sexual subservience. What comes through most strongly from soft pornography is a generalized but universally codified need of women – to verify the reader's existence, to affirm his desirability, to secure for him a sense of his own desire.

Women's complicity is a conceit fundamental to the workings of soft pornography. Without it the whole project would collapse, a tendency which is apparent in the narratives of certain hard core pornography. The assertion of masculine authority – in the sense of power legitimated by the desire of the governed – has given way in hard porn to the symbolic exercise of naked power. Complicity can no longer be relied upon. Women are therefore shown cowering in the face of brute violence, as men assert their domination. The relative security of men's predominance that unifies soft pornography gives way to the shriller and more violent insecurities and paranoias of hard core porn.

The mass production and consumption of soft pornography addresses itself to the unspoken region of men's needs and conflicts. Traditionally, men could be secure in the knowledge that women would be in their place to receive them and to resolve their problems. With women's complicity no longer guaranteed in actual life, soft pornography works to assert that there are no problems. By doing so, it publicly perpetuates a collective lie about women and, as fundamentally, perpetuates the lie that our alienation as men is a natural state that can be magically dissolved in a fuck. In shoring up the structure of traditional masculine authority, soft pornography serves to reproduce the grounds for our continued alienation – a twist that provides the pornographers with high sales and fat profits.

Visiting a sex emporium in New York, Deirdre English commented that the pornography on offer left her with the

> overwhelming feeling . . . of the commercial exploitation of male sexual desire. There it is, embarrassingly desperate, tormented, demeaning itself, taking any substitute and *paying* for it. Men who live for this are suckers, and their uncomfortable demeanour shows they know it.[21]

It is about time the suckers started owning up.

5. Gay machismo

We have no way of knowing what kind of sexual creatures we would be if we had been allowed to grow up in our sexuality. What we do know is that some of us are so fearful, guilty and hung-up that any sexual experience is too threatening, and many of us cope only by hedging it round with restrictions and taboos.

Jane Rule[1]

Gay liberation, before anything else, stands for the integrity and inviolability of sexual desire, the right of men and women to choose their sexual partners according to their needs. No matter how well-intended or how good the end, we can never allow anyone to prescribe our sexuality.

Ken Popert[2]

Style, machismo and effeminacy

Walking into practically any gay pub or club, you can see construction workers, truckers, men in overalls who could be plumbers or electricians, men in bikers' leather, cowboy denims or soldiers' fatigues. Sometimes the image is complete; often men will wear an article of clothing which, by association, links it to the object of desire. Although significantly different from traditional and oppressive images of gay men, are these macho styles a celebration of masculinity which really allows us, as gay men, to distance ourselves from stigma? Are they an attempt to submerge ourselves within heterosexual culture by appearing, on the surface, to be no different from anyone else? What does this development say about our sexuality? What, if any, are the connections with male sexuality as a whole? Why does the desired man appear to be more and more macho?

During the early 1970s gay liberation activists and writers believed that the social distinctions between 'feminine' and 'masculine' could be broken down and an androgynous world would be created within which gender would no longer be relevant.[3] Androgyny was seen as an ideal character which we could all achieve. Social expectations tied to gender would be dropped; all learned distinctions could be removed. Everyone would be encouraged to be gentle, nurturing, co-operative, capable of initiative, sensual, aware of their feelings and attracted to people by their personality and not their physical appearance. An important element in reconstructing the ways in which people could relate was the rejection of sexual objectification of women and men.

Political theories for social change were developed out of experience, practice and theoretical links with feminism and socialist politics. These theories outlined the ways in which our culture could be transformed to create a society in which androgyny was a natural element. Aspects of such ideas have been taken up and diffused throughout our culture. Arguably they are reflected in the style of many young people. Gender appearance amongst a significant proportion of fashion-conscious young people is blurred but this is not, apparently, connected to reversing or changing roles. Effeminacy is still a viable choice for some men and many non-gay men have adopted a softness which can be mistaken for effeminacy. Although make-up and drag form part of the style available to the young there is still a coyness when it comes to defining one's sexuality. 'Swinging both ways' may be more acceptable now but you open yourself to ostracism if you define yourself as gay.

By contrast androgyny is not a popular image among gay men. The 'butch shift' as it has been described by David Fernbach, appears more likely to be a direct response to the popular view that homosexuality involves at a very deep level, a lack of masculinity.[4] Traditionally gay men are supposed to have failed to repress those parts of themselves commonly seen as 'feminine'. This is not a conscious process but one in which, sometimes, we are defined at first by others.

> One could only succeed at establishing manliness, or be a failure, a sissy, someone who couldn't stand up and fight. One didn't choose to be a sissy, a loser – one lost. Since manliness was, of course, what everyone would want, the unmanly must be those who were too weak to make it as a man.
>
> By the time I was in junior high, I defined myself and was defined by other boys as a loser, as the class sissy. Largely this meant that I saw myself as a failed man.[5]

In this way effeminacy becomes an accepted part of homosexuality and forms a part of popular conceptions of gay men. In the film *La Cage Aux Folles I* there is a scene where Renato (the less effeminate one) is attempting to show Albin (an effeminate female impersonator, who in some ways is the strongest character in the film) how to behave like a man. Albin fails and is shown to be incapable of doing anything masculine. Instead of this being celebrated it is depicted both as a loss and a natural consequence of being an effeminate gay.

The apparent masculinity of many gay men, whilst hardly a revolutionary challenge to the gender system, can be seen as a significant challenge to popular assumptions about homosexuality. The shift to machismo has redirected our attention to ourselves as objects of desire and this results in a radical reversal of the self-image of many gay men.[6]

It is easy to see why gay men might assume that it's advantageous to appear butch. It is related to ideas of self-worth and not attempting to disguise sexual attractiveness and images of the erotic. Also it contains an element of 'camp' or self-mockery in reclaiming and using an image which society denies us.

Gay identity

Most of us experience being brought up in families. Even for children in 'non-nuclear' circumstances the ethos of the family is strong. Family life is a process during which we are taught the roles and values of the dominant system. A major tenet of all patriarchial cultures is that male domination of women is the correct way of ordering society. This supremacy is not an automatic characteristic of being male; it is socially constructed in a range of ways and has to be achieved (it is the goal of our youth) and maintained (our task as men). In this way gay men are involved in and experience being brought up as though we were heterosexual. This creates a dilemma within which, although we know that we are not heterosexual, we accept that we are men like any other and often behave as such. A fundamental part of gay liberation was consciousness raising, which involved deeply questioning our behaviour towards each other and towards women. Even if we did not treat women as sexual objects we were not exempt from expecting them to service our needs and relegating them, along with gay men, to the status of second class citizens.

All the time we are being taught that gay feelings towards other men are socially unacceptable and invalid. The resultant self-oppression makes it hard, though not impossible, for us to assert that our sexuality is positive:

> In our society the depiction of sexuality is *always* in heterosexual terms, and any affirmation of homosexuality is an attack on prevalent values. Hence to declare the validity of homosexuality, to reject the judgement that it is sick, evil, a maladjustment, a deviance, a perversion, is a political statement, and the assertion of a homosexual identity is as much a political act as was the assertion of a Czech or Romanian identity in the nineteenth century.[7]

Self-oppression works the same way for gay men as it does for women.

To be homosexual is not necessarily to be gay. To assert that you or I am gay is to take on an identity the starting point of which is an attraction, emotional and/or sexual to those of your own sex. Thus gayness is a *social form* of homosexuality, whilst homosexuality is a part of sexuality, available to all, which manifests itself in a variety of ways. This appears consistent with the Freudian analysis of a polymorphous and undifferentiated sexuality. Whilst Freud can be criticised for his misogyny and his strong belief in the uses of therapy to keep us 'normal', his views on the development of male sexuality through conditioning are potentially much more useful than a belief that we are born with our sexuality intact.

Before the gay liberation movement the homosexual was seen, if male, as the expression of the feminine; the 'camp' man. This is still true within societies where to be fucked is seen as being less than male whilst the man who fucks is not necessarily viewed as a real homosexual at all.

> Opinion generally was that homosexuality consisted of older men taking younger boys as female substitutes. When a man seduced a youth I don't think people regarded it as a homosexual act. It was a homosexual situation satisfying a heterosexual need.[8]

So says an elderly homosexual recalling the attitudes of his youth. This particular attitude is the popular application of traditional gender roles which see the *real* man as a penetrator. Defining yourself as gay means that you have to move out of the heterosexual world you are born into. The family process encourages us to conform to traditional views of gender. If we are male we are taught not to cry, to repress our feelings and desires, in return for a slice of the patriarchial cake. Gay men are caught in the double bind of being told that we are not men yet being expected to behave as men.

Early studies of sexuality encouraged the view that homosexuality was congenital – a direct result of a combination of female and male characteristics in a body resulting, for men, in a 'feminine soul in a male body', as K. H. Ulrichs defined it. This belief in the biological basis of gender is apparent in his work and in that of sociologists Henry Havelock Ellis and Magnus Hirschfeld. These early pioneers have influenced general social attitudes even to this day. A distinct idea was generally developed which asserted that male homosexuals should be divided into 'passive' or 'active'. The active type was seen as forceful and penetrative, rejecting in himself any signs of femininity and seeking as an emotional/sexual partner the passive type. This 'invert' would be gentle, wishing to be pursued; he would be likely to adopt 'pseudo-feminine' mannerisms. This idea comes close to the stereotype upheld by the sissies of the Hollywood films of the 1920s, 30s and 40s and in many television plays and sitcoms of today.[9] These became the accepted stereotypes.

During the early 1970s a common feature of coming out (and this is still true today) was stories of how gay men knew they were different in their feelings towards other men. But they didn't define themselves as homosexuals because they didn't conform to the popular image, or else they understood that they loved men and that the popular conceptions were wrong. It is only through meeting and being with other gay men that we come to accept the parts of ourselves which are close to the stereotypes. With other gay men it is alright to be camp, you are given the support to explore yourself within a subculture, away from the condemnation of society. Similarly in meeting and being with other gay men we may overturn the popular conceptions that we have grown up with. In my youth I assumed that because I was the younger partner it was my role to be fucked. The first time my lover expressed a desire to be fucked by men I was shocked but from then on, I realized that gay men are capable of enjoying a variety of roles.

The gay liberation movement challenged these notions of homosexuality. 'Glad to be gay' means that we affirm a sense of ourselves as being of worth, regardless of how we are categorized within society. Gay writers provided an alternative to traditional ideas of gender division. In *The Spiral Path*, David Fernbach develops these ideas to show the process gay men experience under patriarchy:

> To define yourself as gay, however, even in the minimal sense of accepting the judgement of society that there is something different about you, is to recognize that your homosexuality has something about it that is radically incompatible with the prevalent normality – that you are 'bent', 'queer', i.e. in no way a proper man. And given that the normal masculinity reproduced by the gender system leads automatically to a preferentially hetero-sexual choice of partner, a preferentially homosexual choice is quite rightly interpreted as a sign of a certain lack of masculinity.[10]

The shift towards macho style appears to give the lie to the idea of gay men as effeminate. But is this really so? David Fernbach argues that 'gay men . . . really are effeminate'. But he does this, not in the reductionist sense of the early gay movement of being 'non-masculine', but by showing that gay men belong to a group of men who have failed to complete a course in masculinization. Early theory, as expressed in articles in *Come Together*, an early gay liberation paper, represented an attack on traditional roles. It implied that the challenge of those roles, by living out a combination of elements from both female and male roles (usually referred to as 'gender-fuck') would result in liberation. Fernbach's analysis is more complex. We as gay men are some of the most visible drop-outs (as are a few non-gay men) from the social construction of masculinity. Sometimes we progress a long way through the course before we drop out – we marry, have children – or else we realize who we are much earlier. At some stage we decide to build our lives around the fact that we are men loving men; we reject being labelled as masculine.

As we grow up we each, individually or with support from others, deal with various forms of oppression ranging from the edicts of orthodox religion to instructions from parents and teachers not to walk *that* way, not to talk *that* way, to become successful competitive men. We cannot take seriously the staple references to masculinity, and instead develop our own images of how we want to be – images which will, at any given point in time, satisfactorily resolve the question of what being a man means. Hopefully, we at least have enough resolve to ensure that we keep on going; but the pressures on us to be truly male are so great that a substantial proportion of us never make it. The importance of the question 'what is a man?' and our need to answer it should not be underestimated. After all, many men spend their whole lives ensuring that they have the word 'excellent' on their reports for masculinity.

If the position of gay men within the gender system is one of subordinated masculinity, then that is a position which tells us that we are not real men, and which tries to hide us. So an exaggerated masculine style (as also an exaggerated feminine style) is one of a probable series of responses. This results in us knowing that we are men who love men who live in a society that refuses to recognize this in any positive way. We are depicted as less than men, subordinated within the patriarchial culture. Now we have emerged not only as effeminate but in a way that underlines the absurdity of masculine images whilst affirming our self worth as men. It is particularly ironic that these images contain, for some of us, a highly charged eroticism. Adoption of masculine images can, for some of us, feed into our sexual desires and fantasies; we focus on ourselves as subjects of desire rather than on the straight man, who may be viewed as unobtainable. This can be true even if we are aware of the contradictions of the macho image.

Two images of surface masculinity have reached the level of stereotypes on the social scene for gay men. One is the clone – check shirt, faded blue jeans, bovver boots, short hair and moustache. The other is the all-leather or denim man. Of course not everything is clear-cut, and blurring of images occurs all time. The clone may ring the changes within the basic framework of jeans and workshirts but the image always stays within the bounds of respectability, unlikely to cause offence or attract adverse comments. The leather man is treading more dangerous ground. Black leather is saturated with sexual meaning. It has layers of implication; the wearing of it is to enhance sexual desirability through an indication of strength and power; it is not soft to look at but it is when touched or caressed. The difference between looking (and the meanings conveyed by this) and caressing (and the meanings conveyed by that) are part of its allure. Allure as an object of eroticism that heightens the potency of the subject of desire.

Leather acts as a stimulus to fantasy and suggests a cameraderie bolstered by images of strength. The leather is specific; the jackets are the type worn by bikers and the association with a powerful machine held between one's legs is not, for all its crudity, to be dismissed. The basic costume of the jacket can be built upon in a highly fetishistic manner until every item adorning the body is made of leather. Leather men often belong to specific clubs as well as being members of the general gay scene. Their sexual image of potency is spread throughout gay literature and is a standard element within male gay erotica.

These are two of the standardized images and like all stereotypes, they obscure reality. It is rare to find anyone who lives up to the standard image. The same can be said for effeminate men; although they have 'camp' in common they use discernably different styles. Within the gay scene there are a series of styles which may use elements from any one of these images. These range from men who on the surface appear masculine, but do not live out the traditional notions of the male role, to men who use traditional masculine notions and scenarios of power in their sexual practice.

This fails to include men, like myself, who do not (or try not to) adopt such images in terms of dress or manners but who may, as I do, have fantasies of sexual desire focused on men who visually conform to current images of masculinity. Not only in sexual fantasy but when cruising I may be more interested in satisfying erotic desire with a butch-looking man; this does not, however, mean that the sexual experience itself will conform to the notions of 'passive' and 'active'. What is consistent within all of this is seeing particular forms of the male body as erotic.

There is an inherent contradiction within such sexual objectification: exaggeratedly masculine men are 'camp', for no matter how much any gay man may approximate any image of traditional masculinity, he is still a gay man. And as a gay man is still open to being a scapegoat for the fears of others.

Clark Henley in *The Butch Manual* presents this contradiction clearly for it is not only a manual to be used by those wishing to adopt a macho image – it also sends up that image. He argues that the attainment of such an image results in a negation of self:

> The key to developing Butch is simplicity, a concept which does not particularly abound in the gay community. Empty the mind – keep it that way. Butch is pure, Butch is direct, Butch is less, much less. No extra-curricular gestures in physical movement. We are *not* interested in biographical body language. No enticing restrictive clauses, dubious dangling participles or overachieving irrelevant modifiers in conversation. We are *not* interested in wading around in exclamation points. Taste and breeding are functions of learned behaviour. Butch is more a function of amnesia.[11]

This point of view undercuts the 'taking itself seriously' aspect of machismo. But it fails to explain the attractiveness of the image, even though it clearly indicates that the surface impression is one of immobility, lack of expression. This is consistent with it being an attempt to portray stereotypical masculinity; but what is the attraction of this? It may be romantic to wish to be the one man who disturbs the impenetrable gaze, but the inescapable reality is that these men do meet and make love with many men.

Sex and Image

I was taken to my first gay pub when I was 16 and my first gay club when I was 17; both were in the town near where I then lived. They were the only meeting places for gays other than the streets, parks and 'cottages' (toilets). The most common place for gays to meet is the gay pub, for clubs are not to be found in every town. Pubs are places to be seen in as well as places to hide in. In smaller cities or towns they are likely to contain greater variety in the styles people adopt; camp queens mixing with leather queens and clones. In larger cities, the larger number of pubs usually mean that many cater for specific groupings within the subculture. But in one way all gay meeting places are the same; they function for some people as places to meet someone for sex. Rituals of cruising exist even in the least cruisy pub.

The delight in having sex with men we don't know and from whom we demand nothing except reciprocal physical pleasure involves a desire to obtain a comradeship with men that isn't based on the male bonding of rank, hierarchy and competition. The possibilities for creative sexual behaviour are ones which gay men are able to explore. These sexual expressions are not merely a matter of taste, though taste is an important part of sexual play, but rather are a combination of the effects of our upbringing and the pressures of life now.

Gay male sexual practice can, in reality, be problematic, for the objects of our desire, when freed from heterosexist assumptions, are not free from the cultural rag-bag we all carry around with us. We too have romantic illusions, experience fragility in maintaining relationships over long stretches of time and have fears which affect the ways in which we relate to each other. Sex with strangers may be enjoyable but there is often some form of aftermath experience – either discovering that we have absolutely nothing in common and cannot extend communication beyond the physical, or realizing that we do share more than a physical expression of needs. Another factor can be the environment in which sex takes place. The experience is cognitively different if it happens in a grimy back alley rather than a warm and comfortable room. Despite our dreams, we cannot remove ourselves from the world we are in and consequently our hopes and expectations are always precariously balanced. Love may be an aim, it is not always the result.

Gay male sex has always involved elements of ritual, a ritual which often underlines the relationships of power in our society. Once in bed or wherever sex is taking place, neither partner may be more dominant, more in control, but the process of getting there involves a subtle play with dominance and submission. John Rechy has written elegantly about the cruising dances which take place in clubs, pubs, parks, and streets. [12] Fantasy is an important element – the clothes, the lighting, the body stance. Even a darkened space inhabited by many bodies is awash with fantasy stimulated by the senses of smell, taste, touch and hearing.

Because of the increased awareness of our sexuality, more and more gay men are expressing a desire to explore parts of ourselves which we have kept hidden. Greater discussion of our sexual practice, our mores and morals encourages us to acknowledge denied areas of our psyche. Certainly I would not have done anything about realizing my own sexual fantasies if I had not been supported by debates within the gay movement around areas and forms of sexual expression. A consistent aspect of the writings of the gay movement has been a questioning exploration of our sexual experience and our sexual desires.

The extreme forms of macho image – leather, denim and uniform – are worn by men who enjoy roles. The codes associated with the image indicate quite specifically the sexual practice and desires of the wearer. Many gay men have adopted codes of dress used by people into sado-masochism as style and this has resulted in a lack of clarity, a rather delicious blurring of lines. A gay man may see men in leather, or himself dressed in leather, as erotic but it doesn't mean that he is into s/m sex play. Punks wear bondage gear but that doesn't mean that they act out s/m scenarios.

Because of the increased visibility of the macho man as an idealized sexual image it has become hard to understand the fine distinctions of codified dress. I occasionally wear a set of keys attached to a belt loop on my trousers. Within some gay environments this would be a code signalling, depending on which side I wore them, my liking to be fucked or to be the one who fucks. For years I misunderstood the code. I assumed that wearing them on the right expressed a desire to be the one who fucks and if worn on the left a desire to be fucked. In fact it is the reverse. I know that this association was to do with my seeing the left side as connected symbolically with weakness or powerlessness and therefore that wearing keys on the left fitted in with the male myth that the one who is fucked is less than male. But, as I belatedly realized, it was another example of camp, of gay men overturning straight conceptions and asserting our own sense of reality.

It is confusing if you don't fully understand the codes and as a result imply behaviour or desire that is in contradiction to your intentions. The lack of clarity resulting from the increased use of these codes has been viewed by men heavily into maintaining a butch image as an encroachment to the macho ideal, rather than a source of potential joy. However, for many the attraction of machismo is an acceptable way of openly celebrating the eroticism of the male body. It is a safe eroticism in that the images of desire are often those endorsed as desirable by society in general; though not endorsed as desirable by men for men. Strong, solid, clearly identifiably masculine men but with a difference – a camp difference.

Within these images of eroticism there is a consistent theme of strength and gentleness. Even in the 'hardest' man a hint of warmth or caring deepens the eroticism. In my dreams the sex usually ends with me in his arms aware of the strength, experiencing the gentleness and caring. It is the kiss after orgasm, the soft caress that attempts to convey a continuation of knowing. It is a romantic image. Being a sex object has its dangers, as many women are aware. Even if not leading to violence it can be problematic for people often fail to see the personality beneath.

I find male chest hair erotic. The men in my sexual fantasies always have chest hair. When I go cruising I may have sex with an older man who has chest hair rather than with a younger man who doesn't. In the summer it's easier to see which men are hirsute, in the winter I look for tell-tale signs at the base of the neck, backs of hands or wrists. Yet neither of my regular lovers has that type of chest hair, and neither conforms to popular male images of macho attractiveness. I don't desire them to be different but in my fantasies the men are always strong and gentle. I imagine that if these were the men I really wanted to be with all the time I would seek them out, but my fantasies are objectified; I want the passion, the excitement, the pleasure of skin upon skin and not the lumber of the world.

Conclusion

In seeking an answer as to why traditional images of masculinity are erotic, we should be seeking ways of widening the realms of desire in such a way that we are not trapped into rigid and highly delineated patterns of behaviour suggested by these images. The answer rests in understanding the process by which we become men; the possibility of increasing the range of desire lies in working towards changing that process. By changing that process so that it is not reliant upon a fundamental belief in the divisions of gender, we can create a society in which the roles only become part of sex play, part of the drama of sex and not a straightjacket that prescribes how we behave and operate in the world in general. This not only has implications for gay men but implications for all men.

Traditional images of masculinity are erotic because we are brought up as non-gay men and we redefine our objects of desire as other men. This appears consistent with the idea of gay men being placed in a position of subordinated masculinity which results in us absorbing as objects of desire those images which have the strongest potential within the general culture. Male sexuality is full of the myth of potency; a myth we gay men accept whilst we also know its hollowness. Non-gay men used to be a desired object – our equivalent of the unattainable? – but the 'butch shift' has redirected our attention to ourselves. By creating amongst ourselves apparently masculine men who desire other men we are refuting the idea that we are really feminine souls in male bodies. Gay men can be diverse models of sexual desirability and it is for us to explore and expand that diversity. What we need to be aware of is that the creation of masculine images, whilst subverting heterosexism, is not a radical redefinition of masculinity or a radical attack on the mores of patriarchy. It does hack away at the monolithic façade of patriarchial culture but it cannot end there.

The contradiction of the macho image is that it appears to fit in well with reactionary politics. It is communal within a specific subculture and it also seems individualistic, self-confident and hard. In this way it is a reflection of a wider social context. There is an increasing retrenchment of traditional gender roles in western society and we cannot avoid being influenced by this. The real danger for us is in the macho image being promoted as the only permissible gay image by commercial forces operating within the gay culture. So whilst gay machismo can be a strength in terms of self-affirmation it can lead to a denial of gay politics.

I have concentrated here on the traditional male image used by gay men as an object of desire. Of course effeminate gay men are seen as charged with sensuality and eroticism by many gay men. After all, the radical gay movement would not have emerged in 1969 without the drag queens who led the protests against police harassment. We should celebrate this aspect of our culture, an aspect that can be found within all of us. But we cannot be content with asserting that effeminacy is the answer, as similarly we cannot be content asserting that butch is the answer. All that does is to reinterpret gender divisions within the context of a gay lifestyle. Effeminacy has opened up explorations of gender and male sexuality and placed them in the political arena. Butch images may raise questions about male sexuality but not in the same political sense. However, in redefining masculinity the direction to follow is one which includes gay men who are attracted to or adopt aspects of machismo as an image. This could lead to a redefinition that opens up the image, lays bare the emotions, so that we have an eroticized reality of men who are both gentle and strong, who give full expression to their feelings, listen to their hearts and allow their warmth to be taken, used and reciprocated.

6. Violence and sexuality

In our culture male arousal is a real social problem . . .
Ros Coward[1]

What is it about male sexuality that makes it a social problem? How have we reached the point where violence is automatically associated with men's sexual behaviour and our relationships with women? Rape and battering are hardly new phenomena and it would be difficult to demonstrate in any conclusive way that men are now more violent that ever before. Yet in the last decade male violence towards women has become a central focus of feminist politics and a contentious social issue in all the countries where women's liberation has emerged in any strength. Previously much 'domestic' violence had been hidden because of the deep and long-standing social consensus which viewed the family as an element of cohesion and harmony, rather than as a site of sharp conflict and sexual antagonism.

The silence this consensus has imposed on women has been broken. Feminist organizations like Women's Aid and Rape Crisis have enabled thousands of women to speak out and to escape the violence they have suffered. But men's response to these developments has been muted, to say the least. Where we have begun to think about our own behaviour and how we are implicated in violence, we are often confused, defensive, self-doubting or self-hating and resentful. A challenge to sexual violence may itself produce a further violent reaction.

It has been variously suggested that men's violence is biologically determined, that it is learnt through cultural socialization, or that it is primarily the result of deprivation and the oppressive divisions imposed by the alienated work process of capitalism. Radical feminism has further argued that men are reluctant to confront the problem of violence simply because men enjoy the power it gives us too much.

I don't find any of these arguments very convincing in themselves as real explanations. I want to look at what lies behind them, to see how they might help – or fail to help – our understanding of the problem. It is a huge subject to deal with in a short chapter, and inevitably I have had to truncate arguments, but I hope I have not distorted them. I cannot claim to have found a comprehensive 'answer' to the many difficult questions raised. I hope only to suggest that the problem of male sexual violence is principally that of the deep psychic construction of masculinity within the social and material meanings our culture ascribes to it. A potential for violence becomes encoded in the way we are defined as men and learn to experience ourselves in relation to women. To change this in any fundamental way will require radical shifts not just in the framework of legal protection and sanctions, or even just in sexual attitudes, but also in the organization of child rearing, in household structures, and in employment patterns which reproduce masculinity as it is currently constructed.

I always have a problem in writing about men: should I be referring to 'we' or 'they'? It seems more than a self-indulgent quibble to ask this question. The ideology of masculinity is generalized and pervasive, and moulds us all; but men are not simply passive recipients of it, any more than all women have accepted their own ideological designation. Masculinity as a lived experience is different and rather more complex than the sum of male 'roles', and I will suggest that in this discrepancy, this disjuncture, can be found some of the problems men end up trying to resolve with violence.

To talk as 'we' can suggest a false confessional, a communality of feeling with other men that I don't often share, since I have learnt in quite a self-conscious way to distance myself from and question male assumptions. To retreat into 'they' supposes a spurious separation, a making of exceptions, which men are inclined to use when dealing with uncomfortable political ideas. It also denies the shared experience and understanding which should and does link me with other men.

I remember, several years ago, the first of a difficult series of discussions of violence with the *Achilles Heel* collective. One of us distributed copies of an article from the American radical journal *Mother Jones*, which reported the story of the rape and mutilation of Mary Bell Jones, a teenage girl attacked while hitch-hiking in California. We didn't know how to begin talking about it and found ourselves avoiding each other's eyes. When our reactions came they varied from 'I can't bear to read this', and 'we cannot be expected to take responsibility for these atrocities simply because we are men', to 'we have to accept that at bottom this is what men are about'. It soon became clear that any notion of responsibility was meaningless unless we started from our own violence and our experiences both as perpetrators and as victims, as a way to some understanding of how men acquire such a capacity for brutality. We found it was essential to develop a political analysis of male violence which looked towards possibilities for change, and a concept of personal responsibility not based on guilt but on positive challenge to destructive aspects of masculinity.

One can start such a challenge by asking what lies behind men's silence. We seem to have been unable or willing to say very little about how or why violence is apparently so central to our relationships, our sexual practices and desires. Yet we are nurtured, educated and immersed in a culture whose imagery constantly intertwines violence with sexuality, either subtly or blatantly, and describes each in terms of the other. For evidence of this we only have to look at the covers of pulp thrillers which line the shelves of popular bookshops, the constant stream of 'women in jeopardy' films which are shown in mainstream cinemas, and the cult of video 'nasty'. We might also point to the gradual assimilation of sado-masochism chic into high street fashion and advertising. The meaning of these developments may be uncertain and hotly disputed, but their existence is undeniable.

Some feminists have argued that men's reluctance to question this cultural coupling of sex and violence is simply a conscious calculation of the power it brings – that men know which side their bread is buttered on, and are quite happy to exert control and extort sexual and other services by the use or threat of force. There is an undeniable element of truth in this, yet it seems inadequate as an explanation.

Men mostly do grow up in selfish expectation of being serviced by women, but they also grow up with expectations of breadwinning, work, family duties and responsibilities. Although ideas about marriage have changed considerably over the last 20 or 30 years the marriage contract is still very widely regarded both by men and women as a reciprocal agreement – a bargain. Research on the distribution of family income, such as that by Jan Pahl,[2] has shown how unequal a bargain financially this often is; men's dependence on the material and emotional support of women is very deep. Nevertheless, it is not clear that the role of 'breadwinner' is automatically such a privileged one, in spite of the oppressive nature of the marriage relationship for many women. Historically, the rigid and oppressive character of most waged labour gave the division between male labour and female servicing a deeply entrenched sense of reciprocity, as both natural and compulsory. The strength of these expectations may have outlived the material circumstances which fostered them, but they are still what underlies the puzzlement and indignation many married men feel when this apparent bargain is challenged.

It is doubtful whether the power to demand or force sexual services from women has led to any widespread sexual satisfaction or happiness amongst men. Surveys in popular magazines and reports from sexologists and sex therapists seem to suggest that anxiety rather than 'cock-sureness' has become a central emotion in male (hetero)sexuality. A snippet on the women's page of the *Guardian* autumn 1983, provides one example. A telephone advice service, mainly for women with sexual problems, had been set up in a large Italian city—the country commonly thought of as the bastion of self-confident male machismo. In the first few months, it was flooded with calls from men in desperate doubt and anxiety about their inability to 'perform' sexually and to live up to their own image of masculinity.

Women's liberation, the growing assertiveness of women with a bit more money and power in the world, is popularly blamed for the wave of male impotence and insecurity that is reported. It seems possible that much contemporary violence against women does result from the challenge women pose to male self-esteem; it could be argued that men are only confused and unhappy because their power is being challenged. But this only raises more questions: what is this masculinity which is so powerful and dominant but also apparently so fragile and vulnerable to challenge? How does a sexuality commonly understood as naturally predatory and aggressive become so set about with doubt and failure?

Violence as male supremacy

In attributing male violence to a conscious and systematic attempt by men to maintain women's social subordination, radical and revolutionary feminists have asserted a universal and trans-historical system of male supremacy in which power is defined by rape, battering and murder. The growing pornography industry is cited as the propaganda arm of the 'patriarchial' system.

It is not surprising that this stark picture of society has achieved prominence, for it corresponds to the deep anger many women feel towards men for the atrocities that they themselves and other women have suffered. It has been a salutory and enlightening experience for men to have felt this anger directed at them. But although the analysis of male violence has inspired a militant and combative activism, the issue is a great deal more problematic if we really expect and hope that anything will change. I cannot discuss here general problems with theories of patriarchy, but I want to make a few points about rape and pornography which I think are relevant.

Susan Brownmiller, in *Against Our Will: Men, Women and Rape*[3] first set out the ground for the idea of rape as a universal system of control. She collected a wide range of persuasive supporting evidence for this theory from different historical periods and from different cultures. The main problem with her argument is that by retaining the viewpoint and the interpretive framework of her own late twentieth-century culture, she fails in the end to distinguish the historical and cultural specifics of others. It then becomes difficult to understand the meaning of any differences which do exist. There is admittedly a danger on questions like rape of falling into a liberal relativism in respect of other cultures – but there are other approaches. Anthropologist Peggy Reeves Sanday, for example, has suggested that there are a number of cultures where rape is quite unknown.[4] Julia and Herman Schwendinger have further argued that the prevalence of rape in societies where it is known seems closely correlated to general social antagonisms and to the extent to which different societies are hierarchically organized.[5] This does not in itself contradict the idea that rape may be one form of the exercise of power and control; clearly it is one almost exclusively practised by men. But it does suggest that in order to understand it we need to concentrate less on its supposed universality and more on the specific features which seem to generate it in particular societies and particular historical periods.

A similar problem exists in radical feminist approaches to pornography. Anti-pornography campaigners, both in the USA and England, have asserted an unquestionable link between the consumption of pornography and actual violence against women, even though the connection between fantasy, representation and practice is far from being clearly understood. It has become difficult to challenge this orthodoxy, although some feminists both in England and the USA have begun to do so.[6] I doubt whether pornography can be 'read' as a simple description of male sexuality or even of male fantasy (though it is interesting to see how it seems to shape the language and forms within which male fantasy is expressed.)[7] If it says anything coherent at all about male sexuality it seems to be more about passivity or the fear of passivity in the face of the threatening reality of sex. Real erotic feeling dissolves and disintegrates into the solitary pursuit of the illusory substitute offered by the captured and static imagery, and the creams, potions and paraphernalia of techno–phallocracy.

Andrea Dworkin has tried to generalize and universalize a 'history' of pornography in its function as propaganda for patriarchy.[8] Although we can accept that graphic and written material depicting sexual imagery and activity has been in circulation in many different cultures at different times, it is hard to see how we can accept any single meaning or significance in this material. Dworkin and other anti-pornography campaigners base their assertions primarily on the specific form of violent imagery presented in some contemporary hard core porn, but the availability of this type of material and the mass consumption of soft porn are both recent and specific historical phenomena which require a corresponding social explanation beyond ahistorical concepts of male supremacy.

To question these assumptions is not to deny that there is a link between male sexuality, violence and women's subordination. A woman on her own at night in a quiet street has no reason to be confident that the man walking behind her will not harass or attack her. The woman clerk or junior executive cannot always be sure that her boss will not use his position to force sexual advances on her. But to say that all men are rapists must be to define all heterosexual activity, in a society where women are subordinate, as rape, and all heterosexual women as victims. It is possible to argue this, but then rape loses any specific meaning at all. In this argument, all contradiction, all sense of change and development, are denied. It is a static and monolithic picture of society which itself belongs in a curious way to the same timeless and decontextualized zone which is the realm of pornography. Men and women alike are fixed frozen in the same depersonalized tableau of aggressor and victim. All the cultural explanations in the world cannot disguise the biological determinism that lies at the heart of such a theory. In the end it becomes a let-out for men rather than any real challenge. As Vic Seidler says:

> In a strange way the idea [that all men are rapists] can leave many men untouched as they accept this judgement of themselves intellectually. They can credit themselves with supporting the women's movement while not really having to challenge themselves.[9]

Violence as innate aggression

Our biology is still, of course, most commonly regarded as the determinant of sexual violence. Male sexuality is seen as an innate, aggressive 'drive' – a natural legacy of biological evolutionary imperatives of our descent from animality. Culture and environment may be given some credit, but the image of the 'naked ape' still lies at the heart of bourgeois sexual morality. These assumptions about sexual differences between men and women have an ancient lineage, but they were given an important secular and scientific backing in the evolutionary theories of Charles Darwin.

Darwin's study of natural selection in the plant and animal world convinced him that women's evolutionary role was to restrain the animal urges of men (which tended perpetually to threaten human progress towards civilization) and re-channel them into family life. This gave a scientific rationale for the double standard of female chastity and male philandering so characteristic of nineteenth-century bourgeois morality. This model of male urgency and female receptivity still persists despite a wider acceptance of women's own sexual needs and pleasures, and the boundary between rape and mutual sexual activity remains blurred because of it.

The idea of natural male aggression has earlier roots also in the seventeenth century philosophy of Thomas Hobbes. He portrayed man as violent, essentially individualistic and competitive in the selfish pursuit of his objectives. Elizabeth Wilson has pointed out that what Hobbes philosophized as nature was in fact more a description of a particular society in transition from feudalism to mercantile capitalism, and that the violence and aggression Hobbes saw was both a product of and a justification for the morality of the times.[10]

Hobbes's pessimistic view of life as 'nasty, brutish and short', and of self-interest as the guiding human motivation, has always been the philosophic base for right-wing economic liberalism. More recently it has also provided the basis for the social and moral onslaught of the new right, especially in the USA. Barbara Ehrenreich has produced a fascinating analysis of what she describes as the 'flight from commitment' in the changing roles and styles of men in American society since the 1950s.[11] She shows how the new 'moral majority' have mobilized as much against these changes in men as against the achievements of feminism. It is in precisely Hobbesian and Darwinian terms that the new right issue warnings about the social consequences of a mass collapse of gender roles. Ehrenreich quotes George Gilder, a leading new right activist and writer: 'The crucial process of civilization is the subordination of male sexual impulses and psychology . . .'[12] Gilder argues that men's nature must be controlled and channelled by women as dependent wives into the socially useful breadwinning role. The single man who fails to marry and take on this role should be regarded not just as selfish or immature but as positively criminal:

> The single man in general is disposed to criminality, drugs and violence. He is irresponsible about debts, alcoholic, accident-prone, and venereally diseased. Unless he can marry, he is often destined to a Hobbesian life – solitary, poor, nasty, brutish and short.[13]

It is not hard to see why the neo-Hobbesian discipline of 'socio-biology' has drawn support from the right in its efforts to reassert the leading role of genetic and biological imperatives in gender behaviour. Much of the scientific evidence used and the conclusions drawn have been shown to be dubious to say the least. The conclusions we can usefully draw for human behaviour from observation of captive sticklebacks seems distinctly limited, as Elizabeth Wilson has pointed out. Yet it is this kind of experimentation which makes up Konrad Lorenz's famous *On Aggression*, often quoted as evidence of man's innate aggressive tendencies.[14]

In the end what matters is not that, scientifically, most of these ideas don't bear much scrutiny, but that they have filtered down into commonsense notions which shape the way men and women interpret their own actions and feelings. Elizabeth Wilson says:

> Biology becomes a giant moral let-out. Such arguments are popular because they pander to our inertia. After all, to change one's behaviour involves pain and effort. It's much easier to pretend to be a baboon.[15]

And it is, of course, as a kind of human baboon or 'naked ape', unable for a moment to contain his 'urges', that the rapist or batterer is generally portrayed in the popular press and, with monotonous regularity, in the pronouncements of learned judges.

Violence as a response to the environment

Conservative ideas of innate aggression have often been opposed by the left, marxist and social democratic alike, with an argument that violence and aggression are primarily responses to an objectively threatening and brutalizing environment. It has clearly been a progressive and optimistic argument in that it suggests that change is possible and achievable. But Marxism's tendency to reduce social problems to economics has, at its crudest, spawned absurdities like the Socialist Workers Party's initial analysis, in their weekly paper, of the Peter Sutcliffe 'Yorkshire Ripper' murders as a product of unemployment.[16]

Even on a more sophisticated level, the sociological analysis of cultural and environmental causality, on which post-war reform has been based in this country and other western democracies, has been severely limited by its basic commitment to gender as biologically given and un-problematic. Sociologists and radical criminologists have rightly warned against being stampeded by moral panics into assuming that violence, including sexual violence, is running out of control. Difficulties of comparison with other periods, and changing fashions in reporting, make any evidence inconclusive, but it may be the case that violence between individuals is actually less common now than in the late nineteenth century. Mass education, some redistribution of wealth, better housing, health services, divorce reform and political enfranchisement have all clearly contributed to the transition from the society of Zola's *Germinal*, from the murky and dangerous London of Dickens and Mayhew, and from Sinclair's brutal Chicago.

But projects of social reform in England, the USA and Europe have been closely wedded to the notion of the family as a locus of private relations lying, apparently, outside the scope of political intervention. Whatever the origins of this separation of 'public' and 'private' – generally ascribed to the development of capitalist wage labour, or to the penetration among the working class of the bourgeois model of family life – this division is increasingly ideological rather than actual. The state has intervened politically in ways that impinge on every aspect of personal relationships and the family – from the establishment of family planning clinics to old age pensions, taking in divorce reform and social security, the growth or reduction of nursery places, and the power of the social services to remove children from parents. But still these interventions have been presented as necessary but limited incursions on to territory properly belonging to the individual or the private family. This enduring vision of the family as a private 'haven in a heartless world', the place, within a programme of social reform, where children grow 'straight and tall' is precisely the cause of the invisibility of violence against women – and against gay men. The idea that male aggression and violence are products of a brutalizing environment and will disappear with the advent of ameliorative social reform has been entirely undermined by this commitment to the family as unproblematic and naturalistic, even though the family is the place where gender characteristics are first acquired, then fostered and reproduced.

Violence as learnt activity

In the late 1960s the sociological and political consensus on the family began to come under attack from various quarters, including that of R. D. Laing and the anti-psychiatrists, and that of resurgent feminism. Since then the concept of 'socialization' has come to be used extensively to analyse the process of gender acquisition. The great value of this work has been in its ability to break from notions of gender as given, and to examine how gender characteristics which reflect social norms are learnt. Studies have shown how children are influenced by the idealist representation of family values in children's books, school textbooks, and other cultural imagery. These ideas are reinforced by gender-differentiated practice in child care and education, by the dominant representation in public imagery of a naturalistic gender division of labour, and by peer group pressure. There has been relatively little specific study of the formation of masculinity within this perspective, although Andrew Tolson's work shows clearly how decisive the influence of work and work expectations is on men and boys.[17]

But violence is not just learnt as male activity. It is part of what actually shapes the contours of masculinity. Vic Seidler describes how violence becomes encoded with boys' bodily stances:

As boys, we have to be constantly on the alert to either confront or avoid physical violence. We have to be ready to defend ourselves. We are constantly on our guard. This builds tension and anxiety into the very organization of our bodies. You get so used to living with it it comes to feel normal. Masculinity is never something we can feel at ease with. It is always something we have to be ready to prove and defend.[18]

The coercive nature of this process must be emphasised. It is not optional – all boys in our society have to go through it to some degree. Julian Wood's research on boys suggests that the traditional assumptions of characteristics of masculinity are widely and deeply ingrained at an early age.[19] Yet not all boys fall so clearly into these patterns. Some find themselves, as young gay men increasingly do, resisting this socialization and the assumptions on which it is based. The fact that some do resist this process, for reasons that are not always clear, throws up one of the difficulties with socialization theory – its implicit functionalism.

The mechanics of socialization presuppose the influence of a body of predetermined ideas and roles which equip the subject to take a particular functional position in society. But how are these roles and functions determined? Traditional sociology has suggested that they have evolved as a contribution to the harmonious workings of society, but this view has merely served to obscure and conceal the existence of conflict, as I have already argued.

Proponents of the 'male supremacy' thesis might argue that male socialization serves men's own interests. Men have certainly come to hold and defend power as men in society, even when their class or racial positions renders them relatively powerless, but men seem increasingly to be reaching the conclusion that power is often wielded at considerable expense to their own humanity. This does not necessarily always include a recognition of how women are oppressed in this power relationship. It is a contradiction which Barbara Ehrenreich has emphasized when she argues that much of the shift in male sex roles in the USA has been caused less by feminism than by men seeking to shrug off self-oppressing aspects of traditional male roles.

Marxists have traditionally held the view that gender socialization is demanded by the needs of capital, and there is considerable evidence to support this view. Gender divisions, particularly the gender division of labour, have become deeply embedded within capitalist ideology and the economic and social policies of capitalist nations. The family, and familial ideology, has in certain senses been extremely efficient at reproducing class and gender relations, servicing and reproducing a workforce, and at organizing and maximizing consumption. Andrew Tolson's work, as mentioned, supports the view that the demands of capitalist production are deeply influential on the formation of masculinity.

Nevertheless, there are many aspects of sexual divisions which are hardly inherent in the logic of capitalism. Even though it has been recognized that sexual divisions in the working class have weakened its ability to mount a resistance to capitalism, masculinity has also been crucial to the traditions of this resistance. Men's propensity for violence is not just against women but also in areas such as street violence, football hooliganism, and the 'problem of youth' (really the problem of *male* youth); these forms of violence can specifically be seen as positively dysfunctional for the capitalist state.

Michele Barrett has pointed out that socialization theory also has problems in explaining and incorporating the variations of sexual practice because its main mechanism is seen as social pressure to conform.[20] Studies of sexual behaviour from the famous Kinsey Institute reports of 1948 and 1953 up to more recent work, such as that of Shere Hite, have suggested that surprisingly little conformity in sexual practice actually exists beneath apparent conformity to gender expectations.[21]

In the Hite report on male sexuality large numbers of men described practices and feelings which it would be extremely difficult to encompass within a unitary notion of male sexuality based on potency, unemotionality, predatory desire, dominance and control. If we are to see men as functionally socialized into roles as workers, breadwinners, soldiers, power wielders, how are we to explain the widespread occurrence of homosexual practice (distinct here from homosexual identity), male masochism, and a whole range of practices which fall outside of the pattern generally associated with proper male socialization?

At the same time, it is also true that the majority of men interviewed listed most of these attributes as essential to their ideas of being a proper man. They regarded intercourse as still the central and most important part of sex (even though, for many it was not the most pleasurable) and felt that they did not have sex often enough. These comments are fairly typical:

> I have to take to bed as many women I can, as often as I can, the more often the better, to be a real man.
>
> I am ashamed to tell you how often I have intercourse, it is so infrequent.
>
> Of late the frequency is rare, my wife does not have the drive I have.[22]

It appears that men still absorb the accepted ideas of what sex is supposed to be, even if it does not necessarily correspond to their own experiences and their own practices; so it would be wrong to suggest a clear break between gender socialization and sexual practice. There are nevertheless discontinuities which I believe are important and which have perhaps widened as personal relationships and sexuality have become more and more a matter of public interest and enquiry. What we are seeing may be partly a variation among men reflecting uneven shifts and changes in sexual attitudes in the face of feminism and the 'sexual revolution'. More than that there seems to be a tension within masculinity itself – a tension between the compulsive and regimenting demands of masculine socialization and the desire to express a variety of needs and emotions which may run counter to this socialization, and often have little intrinsically to do with sex at all. As Andy Metcalf has put it:

> Wanting to have sex a lot, feeling a great need for it, is often quite tied up with misery. There's no direct link between feeling sexy, feeling erotic, having desire for someone else, and wanting sex . . . I think sex is a vehicle for many needs and feelings; making things better when you're feeling tense, anxious; feeling out of contact with somebody and out of contact with yourself. It's the easiest way to connect to somebody and to yourself.[23]

This is not in itself gender specific. Women too learn to channel a variety of non-erotic needs and feelings into sex. But for men it becomes heavily charged because of the emotional illiteracy which is part and parcel of male socialization. So often sex then becomes a bottleneck of pent-up and misdirected yearnings, frustrations and anger The pressure of this mass of undigested and unexpressed emotion which clusters around sexuality is perhaps what gives the myth of male urgency its subjective power for men. Relationships with women are really the only socially permitted area for uncircumscribed expression of male emotion and vulnerability, in so far as this is permitted at all. But although there is now more general public acceptance of the idea that men should be able to express emotion more openly, the communication of this emotion in relationships with women can become a minefield where there is little shared language of emotionality and little subjective experience in common.

Despite legislative regulation of sexuality, bourgeois ideology defines the act of sex as essentially a private one, where two people meet in 'free exchange', casting off the world with their clothes and becoming anonymous, lost in oneness with their partners. In fact, nothing could be further from the truth. Angela Carter remarks:

> No bed, however unexpected, no matter how apparently gratuitous, is free from the de-universalizing effect of real

life. We do not go to bed in simple pairs; even if we choose not to refer to them, we still drag there with us the cultural impedimenta of our social class, our parents' lives, our bank balance, our sexual and emotional expectations, our whole biographies – all the bits and pieces of our unique existences.[24]

Still it is not only the social, economic, or even physical power inequality between women and men which is the problem. Social and physical power gives men license to resolve conflict and contradiction by force, but it is not in itself the root of this violence. More fundamentally, it is the process of gender construction which creates in men a deeply ambivalent feeling towards women. Nancy Friday subtitled her collection of men's sexual fantasies 'The Triumph of Love Over Rage'. This might be considered as an unreasonably optimistic conclusion to have reached, but it does express the ambivalence of men's feelings. To see what this ambivalence is and how it arises I feel we can usefully look to more recent explorations in psychoanalysis and the physical construction of gender.

Illusions of independence

Feminists and socialists have approached psychoanalysis in recent years in two ways. First, in a personal way, as an attempt to grapple with conflicts in our own lives, as apparently intractable patterns of feeling which have been rejected intellectually seem to resurface again and again. Secondly, in an attempt to understand the place these feelings have in the construction of gender. As a project it has not been without its problems. Michele Barrett has usefully discussed the difficulties of reconciling psychoanalysis and materialism.[25] She points out the applicability and the historical specificity demanded by a materialist approach, and how it occupies a cloudy zone between the biological and the social, where any kind of synthesis with feminism or Marxism is highly problematic.

While accepting these serious limitations, I want to suggest that the psychoanalytic framework can still shed some useful light on how the psychosocial construction of masculinity in a capitalist society predisposes men towards sexual violence.

In Freud's account of a boy's sexual development, emotional rejection of the mother is an essential stage in the proper resolution of the Oedipal conflict through which heterosexuality is developed. The consequences of this rejection are not examined as a potential problem except in so far as a failure to reject may result in fixation at a stage of homosexual inclination. Nancy Chodorow has argued that Freud undervalued the importance of the mother/daughter relationship and the crucial role it has in transmitting the qualities of nurturing, which reproduce the social aspects of mothering and other activities which society associates with mothering.[26] I want to suggest that the rejection of the mother by the son under the social pressures which draw him towards the external world of the father (or of men, whether the father is actually present or not) has also been given too little consideration. We do not have to see this process as universal or transhistorical. Anthropologists have found enough evidence from other cultures to suggest that this particular pattern of psychic development is not inevitable. It is the consequence of socially defined gender expectations, and it is in turn the structure through which expectations are reproduced. The tensions within masculinity itself, to which I have referred above, arise because economic and political changes have allowed the possibility of these definitions and expectations to be questioned. Yet the basic problem continues, even if in our society it is not formally marked by the rituals and ceremonials of initiation.

This rejection of the mother, and the relationship of nurturance which binds mother and son together, is in itself a violent and dehumanizing process because it involves an internal rejection and suppression of the son's own potential qualities of nurturing, in favour of the coercive but compensatory attributes held out to him as his reward for achieving malehood. Part of this process is the devaluation in the son's eyes of the gender to whom those rejected qualities are assigned. 'Big boys don't cry' will be drummed into him through his early ears as a constant reminder of his internal struggles: suppression of the language of emotional expression is an inevitable consequence, as Peter Bradbury describes:

> How do we learn in the first place to speak a language of domination? There are many reasons, some of which can be seen if we look at what happens as we go from birth to adulthood. The language we speak to our mothers moves in that time from the most intimate and sensual – the shared utterances of skin and first speech – to the tyrannical, the instrumental and the dismissive. At some time between birth and say 20, we learn to recognize our mothers as servant, nurse, giver of birth – that is, as socially inferior beings from whom, by a process we learn to ignore or disparage, we have somehow sprung. In this conflict between recognition and denial we lose the language of intimacy and the knowledge of our mothers we must have once have had. The reality of the woman who gave us birth and brought us up is reduced in our perceptions to its physicality.[27]

When in adolescence boys begin to re-attach to girls as their 'object-choice', a pattern has been established which makes it difficult to perceive women in any other than an instrumental way. Yet this way of seeing women becomes deeply contradictory. While men expect the service they receive from their mothers, and casually despise women for the inferior status this expectation consigns them to, they find that women now possess unexpected powers of sexual 'attraction'. Women are now also seen to possess arcane skills of emotional intensity and expression – all the feelings men have learnt to deny but which they now look at with some envy. Men start to discover in women an unsettling power which contradicts and undermines their own more obvious social and physical power.

Wendy Holloway has observed how the re-attachment of unconscious feelings about mothers on to women lovers creates a dependence/independence dilemma for hetero-sexual men.[28] Because men are brought up to associate being a man with qualities of independence this dilemma is often resolved by displacing feelings of dependency on to women. Men's vulnerability is thus shielded and the illusion of masculine independence preserved. Holloway goes on to argue that men's fear of dependence and their fear of women's sexuality is associated with anxieties about potential engulfment in unconscious desires for the totality of the mother/child relationship. In this light it is also possible to see that the power women often feel men have in relationship stems in part from men's defensive reaction to these anxieties rather than existing as something innate.

Men nevertheless continue to seek out these dependency relationships, often quite unaware of who is really dependent on whom. Social definitions of women as dependent mean that women too will very often find themselves colluding in this mutual self-deception. But if men's dependence and their emotional weakness within a relationship is exposed and challenged they may well perceive it as a deep threat to their identity and their security. All men's worst fears about themselves and all the ambivalent feelings they have towards women can emerge at these moments, and they may react with defensive hostility or outright violence. It is as though men attempt to exercise, in the only way they know how – by force – the fear of accepting what they are and what they may have lost in the process of becoming what they are.

Within the traditional power structures of the partriarchial family, the areas of power and control men exercise could veil the reality of men's unconscious ambivalence towards women; direct physical control was legitimate and socially acceptable. Social changes such as women's mass entry into the labour market, male unemployment and de-skilling, and the increasing state management of family life, have all tended to undermine the material basis for men's power without fundamentally altering the familial ideological structures within which masculinity is constructed. Faced with this, men may be increasingly inclined to view women as 'too powerful' or dominating. Sexual autonomy or independence shown by women strikes at the heart of this male insecurity and fuels the rage which battles with love.

Amanda Spake, an American journalist, writes about the man who raped and mutilated Mary Bell Vincent:

> What Lawrence Singleton did was to act out a profound, almost mythic rage, an angry fear, a peculiarly male emotion. On that September day, Singleton decided to strike – in his view strike back – at what he perceived to be female domination of his life, his sexuality, his psyche. His acts were sadistic, but his rage is generic.[29]

If we look at the more extreme instances of male violence against women we often expect to find psychopaths and sadists. In reality, research into domestic violence and rape suggests that batterers and rapists are not necessarily specially disturbed, come from all walks of life, and in most respects are ordinary men. What does come out clearly in the Dobash pioneering work, for example, is that the wider the gulf between a man's notion of proper masculine character and behaviour and his own perception of himself, the more likely he is to be violent.[30] The more ill-equipped to deal with these contradictions emotionally, the more likely he will react to any challenge by lashing out. It is a common feature that men become almost amnesiac about violent incidents, as if to admit or recognize them is to see their tenuous security undermined even further. To admit that all they have is physical power is in real terms a confession of absolute weakness.

Similarly, an American study of the psychology of 500 convicted rapists found that few were in any way psychopathic, but that the majority did exhibit certain common characteristics:

[the rapist] is not much in touch with his own needs and feelings, and except for anger his emotional life seems impoverished . . . anxiety and restless dissatisfaction with the existing circumstances of his life and/or with unfulfilled emotional need resulting from a feeling of powerlessness. He feels menaced by his situation and helpless to remedy the situation . . . At the root of all this are deep-seated doubts about his adequacy and competence as a person.[31]

This strikes me as not too unfair a description of the end product of 'normal' masculinity rather than anything unusual or extraordinary. While not all men are overtly violent or coercive towards women, the potential violence within male sexuality is unlikely to disappear in any general and fundamental way as long as men continue to be constructed as emotional illiterates with self-deluding ideas of independence and deep ambivalence between love and fear, attraction and antagonism, towards women.

Where do we go from here?

I have tried to argue that sexual violence is not innate in men in any biological sense, and that it cannot be seen simply as a means of defending men's own power and privilege. It is not a product of capitalism but the consequence of a form of gender construction which is very deeply embedded within capitalist social relations. Where does this leave us – particularly as men? It is not enough to conclude on a note of millenial pessimism that nothing will change till we change the whole world. That's another let-out. We are not cyphers, and we make choices for which we are responsible and should be held responsible.

This is not the place to argue the pros and cons of greater legal sanctions against violent men or to discuss the shortcomings of the penal system. Women need legal protection, safe transport, housing and income opportunities which guarantee their independence. Legal, political, or educational programmes which strengthen women's power to oppose violence should be supported.

How men will change is rather a different question. Men changing their own behaviour is an important starting point, but individual change has only a marginal effect whilst all the material and ideological structures of society are geared towards the reproduction of a masculinity which so often relies on violence to resolve emotional crises or protect fragile egos. One development in collective action by men in the USA which has excited considerable interest in England is counselling for violent men. The American pioneer group in this field is EMERGE. Based in Boston, EMERGE was set up in 1977 with the co-operation of the women's shelter (refuge) network, and the collective of men, including ex-batterers, who run it provide counselling, community education, and training for other agencies. An (as yet) unpublished document puts the position of the collective:

> we are all committed to the principle that serious attack on women abuse must include an equalizing of power relationships between men and women, on a personal as well as a social level. It must also include a challenge to some widely-held stereotypes about what is and what is not appropriate 'male' behaviour.[32]

EMERGE recognize that the initial motivation of many men who come to them for counselling is to re-establish a relationship which has broken down, or to encourage the return of a woman who has left them. Critics of services like EMERGE argue that this rehabilitative emphasis, and its work with men as individuals, fails to tackle the institutional structures which give men social power and which shape the contours of masculinity itself.

It remains to be seen whether projects of this kind will develop in the English context. Clearly there are a great many difficulties and contradictions. But the real potential which does exist in the development of programmes like EMERGE seems to lie not just in the individual counselling of violent men or in the public education, but in the very contradictions such work raises.

To push at and beyond the limitations of individual change in men is to bring us right up against the fundamental construction of masculinity, the sexual division of child rearing which reproduces gender, the employment structures which maintain this division, and the political system which defines our aspirations towards equality. It is also a means to ending oppressive and violent sexuality.

7. Men's sexuality at work

This chapter is about the range of sexual behaviour that men indulge in at the workplace. What appears at first as mysterious, even beyond our control, will be examined as a product of the material circumstances of heterosexual men's alienation and their power over women.

A central contradiction

If I reflect on the connections between my own paid work and my own sexuality I feel uneasy, even embarrassed. Although the connections are strong, there are also emotional (perhaps puritanical) hangovers from my background which say that to acknowledge the possibility of sex whilst at work is to complicate or even denigrate the real purpose of work; on the other hand linking work to my sexuality is to interfere or make impersonal *my* personal sexuality. This expresses a wider view that work should be instrumental and that sexuality should be expressive; to mix them is to offend both.

The phrase 'men's sexuality at work' is a little incongruous. Slaving over a lathe or poring over a deskful of files doesn't seem very sexy. For most men there are two distinct worlds – the public and the private. Sexuality appears at first to reside in the private arena, most obviously during leisure time and in the home. It is as if we are sexual when we are off duty, while workplaces remain concerned with getting the work done.

A slogan from the Paris of May 1968, 'Work – It Will Make You Ugly' says it all.[1] Marx argued that wage labour diminished people: 'the worker feels himself only when he is not working; when he is working he does not feel himself. He is at home when not working, and not at home when he is working.'[2] The worker thus feels his true self, however mistakenly, when he is not at work. Although Marx may have drawn the line between sexuality and work too rigidly (an issue taken up later by Reich, Marcuse and others), he did help to lay the basis for understanding the relationship between the two realms. Following Marx, forms of sexuality could be seen as forms of alienation. Neither sexuality nor work was ever again what it seemed. Both could be understood, at least partly, in terms of the other; but this is not enough to explain male sexuality.

The close relationship of sexuality and work is apparent in the way paid work often forms a major element in men's sense of who they are, including their sense of sexual identity. The ways we talk, walk, flirt, touch and so on are ways of being sexual at work; we use opportunities to show different sexual identities that may be partly work-based. Success at work may be seen as having a sexual element; while failure, demotion or dismissal may produce feelings of inadequacy – 'castration' and 'emasculation'.

Men's sexuality at work thus has a characteristic and rather complex form. In one sense men's sexuality at work is inappropriate, unwanted, inconvenient; in another sense, it is alive, well, and certainly here to stay.

Varieties of sexual behaviour

In some ways, workmates may get to know each other better than domestic or sexual partners. In many places people work alongside or face each other day after day, so that physical and emotional contact may be routine. Indeed such contact may be more continuous than the contact between many husbands and wives, across the breakfast table or at other times.

To link such social contact with sexuality is necessarily to interpret that latter fairly broadly. It certainly involves seeing sexuality as much more than just sexual relationships.

Thus social support and intimacy can blur into sexual feeling and touching, and ordinary conversation, at work and elsewhere, can use and refer to sexuality – as when men discuss women as sexual objects.

Thus, while the dominant view assumes that sexuality can be characterized in terms of its *privateness* with an emphasis on *sexual contact*, the approach developed here is that sexuality can be characterized in terms of its *publicness* with an emphasis on everyday events, *without sexual contact*. Sexuality is used here to refer to all those actions, thoughts and feelings that are related to physical desires for the bodies of others or oneself, not to specifically sexual contact or sexual acts.

In answering the question 'What are the main kinds of sexual behaviour that men engage in at work?' I have drawn on the research done by both women and men, and supplemented it with my own observations and interviews. Much of the writing on sexuality at work focuses on women rather than men; there are some particular aspects of men's sexuality at work, especially between men, that have been very little explored because male sexuality is not seen as being a problem. Similarly most discussion of prostitution focuses on women prostitutes rather than the men kerb crawlers and why they do it.

The vast array of men's sexual behaviour at work can be conveniently described in terms of the following main types: *mutual sexuality*, which may or may not lead to sexual contact and therefore includes dating, mutually agreeable contact and mutual flirting; *exploitation of sexuality*, that involves the use and abuse of sexuality for other, usually economic, ends; *sexual harassment* by men usually of women; and *horseplay*, hearty behaviour usually between men. The first two types can be seen as routine: they tend to be seen as ordinary, even legitimate. The second two types are more bizarre. There is more information available on the questions of mutual sexuality and sexual harassment than the other types, perhaps reflecting the fact that these two are more directly concerned with men's sexual advances towards women.

Mutual sexuality

Places of work provide opportunities for the *search* for mutual sexuality. Such behaviour operates at all levels of intimacy, from the meeting of eyes onwards. It is simply the routine attempt by men to behave sexually in a way that will be mutually acceptable to others, particularly to women. For example, in the course of writing this chapter, I enter a library, the door swings back on its hinges to produce an awful bang. I find myself looking straight at the woman librarian. I smile, look at her eyes and say 'sorry' in mock coyness. It is the most innocent of innocent flirtations and it is gone. The point is, I would smile and say 'sorry' differently to a male librarian.

At the other extreme are fully-fledged searches for, and realizations of, sexual relationships. A survey of 645 readers of the magazine *Wedding Day* found that a quarter had met their marriage partner at work.[3] Thus workplaces provide avenues for sexual advances which, for a time at least, have an element of mutuality about them and which may evolve into long-term arrangements. In other words we are not simply concerned with casual or flirting relationships.

So how do we account for mutual sexuality and the forms it takes? In one sense it could be said that work simply offers convenient numbers of people to each other for some sort of social, and potentially sexual, contact. However, at the same time people at work are usually firmly controlled in terms of where and with whom they work and how they gain access to other parts of the workplace and workforce. Thus a first factor in understanding the development of mutual sexuality is simply the proximity of people to each other at work. In Robert Quinn's survey of 132 romantic relationships at work, the people concerned worked in immediate proximity in 63 per cent of the cases.[4] Romance at work is not random; the chances of falling in love with someone you work with are considerably greater than with someone in the next department. In many workplaces the geographical arrangement involves particular spaces being differentiated in terms of gender, such as the (women's) typing pool, the (men's) factory floor, and the (mixed) reception area. Often this pattern is reinforced by the differential mobility of women and men – women often being relatively fixed at desks, machines, typewriters and counters and men relatively mobile as supervisors, inspectors, professionals and so on. In this way the 'pool' of women that many men come into contact with is likely to be greater than that of men available to women. What this means is that even mutual sexuality arises out of a variety of overlapping work-based considerations – the spatial distribution of workers, the sexual division of labour, the distribution of authority.

A second and clearly highly related factor is that work environments are sites of power, usually of men over women. Men, particularly managers, control the way space and people are arranged. It is often the interstices, the space between spaces, that are less directly controlled and this can provide access between people otherwise confined. These spaces can be of three main types: geographical areas, times during the working day, or social events. The areas include corridors, staircases, lifts, kitchens, passageways, entrance ways, anywhere that people 'bump into' each other. The times include tea breaks, lunchtimes and drinks ('one for the road'), as well as the office party, the Christmas 'do', or the summer outing. Thirdly there are *social events* that take place between people from different departments, sections, even organizations. Sexual behaviour may be more likely in these occasional spaces than in the usual place of work.

In addition, particular men have power over particular women. For example, Quinn's survey found that 74 per cent of romances involved a man in a higher organizational position than the woman. In this sense mutual sexuality may be a half truth, with mutuality superimposed on equality. It is usual for there to be a power differential between those who 'fancy' each other or fall in love, both complicating and giving substance to the relationship. A man may fall in love with an independent, powerful, successful woman, or a dependent, powerless, unambitious woman. It may be much harder to fall in love with a woman at work who is both a peer or colleague, partly because organizations often define women and men differently in the first place, even when they do similar jobs. Furthermore women who become involved, or even assume they are involved, with men in sexual entanglements at work are much more likely than men to suffer by being redeployed, made redundant and so on.[5] Mutual sexuality could be seen as a means of reinforcing the power that men already have over women at work. It is no wonder that many of the texts advising women on how to gain success at work, offer advice such as: 'The worst thing that you can do is fall in love with your boss. If that happens for heaven's sake – GET OUT QUICK!'[6]

In authoritarian work regimes mutual sexuality may be a form of resistance, of 'cocking a snoot' to management, of humanizing an alienating workplace. Another sometimes related feature of workplaces that may encourage mutual sexuality is the level of stress and anxiety. There is considerable social psychological research that connects stress tendencies with romance and even sexual arousal. In these contexts mutual sexuality may be a reaction to alienation at work. On the other hand few workplaces actually seem to encourage mutual sexuality. This can occur directly, as in this description of an organization where romantic relationships were common: 'It was expected that when you hired a secretary, you weren't looking for a typist. In fact hardly anyone could type.' Or it can happen indirectly as when two employees on a summer play scheme became involved with each other 'because they simply had little else to do'.[7] In a few workplaces stress and autonomy can occur together – in effect, a combination of alienation and power. This can be so for those working overtime together or others such as doctors on call, emergency night duty social workers who may even be able to combine living and bedding arrangements with paid work time.

The combination of power and alienation *may limit* the development of mutual sexuality for particular men. Mutual sexuality can bring a variety of sanctions and negative reactions to men. This is especially so as men rise to positions of power in work. Sexuality may be subjugated to other demands such as maintaining status or control. According to a study by Annette Lawson, by the age of 40, 60 per cent of married men and 40 per cent of married women have had 'adulterous affairs'.[8] This contrasts with an American study that '20 per cent of top executives acknowledge having sex outside marriage', and that of these only 8.8 per cent 'reported an affair with a woman in the office'.[9] As men get more powerful the risks get greater.

The other major limitation on mutual sexuality for men is the growing power of certain women, especially as they enter positions of management at work. Women managers can pose a sexual threat to their male peers. Such men 'may avoid contacts with the female office mate [sic] for fear this will cause difficulties at home'.[10] Similar risks may be associated with senior men 'sponsoring' women as potential managers. This, however, is not all, for powerful women can undermine usual tendencies to 'sexualize' women. As a man working under a woman manager put it: 'She's quite well-preserved, I suppose. Quite attractive. But she's so authoritarian, she turns me off.' This comment reinforces conclusions from a study by Mayes of 'female-led groups' in four conferences on nursing and psychiatry:

> When asked to explain their feelings [about the experience of being led by women] men said that they experienced loss of control when every level of their ability to function *as males* came into question. This was particularly important in the area of sexuality – loss of control was revealed to mean loss of sexual control.[11]

Such studies point to a degree of confusion around sexuality where there might previously have been a search for mutual sexuality which was taken for granted. As a man in another American study reported: 'If I had a woman boss, my wife would feel . . . that I was now inferior and not the dominant male that I have led her to believe I am.[12]

Exploitation of sexuality

In contrast to behaviour which is a reaction to alienation at work, the exploitation of sexuality covers the abuse of sexuality. Here sexuality is used as a means to an end rather than as an end in itself. It therefore includes men's appointment and assessment of women on sexual grounds, the use of sexuality in advertising and other public images of work, and the instruction of workers to behave in particular sexual ways towards customers and clients. It involves the blurring of sexuality, often, though not always, sponsored by managements. It can of course turn into harassment but this is sufficiently distinct to warrant separate consideration. It may be possible to bring about a reduction in sexual harassment but not necessarily thereby to reduce sexual exploitation.

Managers can use sexuality as a means of making profit. For example, Lucy Bland and her co-workers write:

> In (some) jobs female sexuality as sexuality on display is part of the *use value of the commodity of labour power itself*. For some secretaries, receptionists, boutique assistants, it is essential to be attractively feminine as well as to serve . . . These women are in effect seeing their own sexuality in the same way that advertising uses women's sexuality to sell other products.[13]

Thus sexuality is a means to an end; business is not worried about sexuality so long as it works. Women and their sexuality are objectified and men are both alienated from and in control of them.

Managers' exploitation of sexuality can also be a means of reinforcing men's power at the same time as making profits. This is apparent in the way secretaries are appointed, assessed and used by managers. Secretaries are frequently treated as conspicuous 'possessions', given all sorts of 'domestic' and protective functions; they act as 'office wives', even clean their bosses' false teeth.[14] The blatantly sexist *Programmed Guide to Office Warfare*, which describes itself as a '. . . witty . . . manual . . . to set about winning power, money and status in your career', encourages such stereotyping and control of women in arguing for choosing the 'best-looking' as against the most competent secretary as follows:

> First, it will make your life more pleasant. Secondly, she will excite the envy of your colleagues. Thirdly, she can be deployed so as to disarm the opposition . . . Suppose you have a favour to ask of another department; you send your beautiful secretary, for who could resist such charm? If you have bad news to impart, again you send the ravishing beauty to calm the savage breast.[15]

By using a secretary's sexuality in this way several things are accomplished at the same time: the furthering of the interests of business and the reinforcement of competition and solidarity between particular men. Secretarial sexuality is not just a matter of directly objectifying women, but is also for the eyes of *other* men. In such ways economic relations and gender relations are intertwined.

Workers' exploitation of sexuality has some similarities and some differences. Cynthia Cockburn provides a wealth of information on this theme and in particular the contradictions that face working-class men employed in the newspaper industry:

> The social currency . . . is women and woman-objectifying talk, from sexual expletives and innuendo through to narrations of exploits and fantasies. The wall is graced with four-colour litho 'tits and bums'. Even the computer is used to produce life-size print-outs of naked women.[16]

This she sees as a development of masculinity within the economic class struggle – 'solidarity forged between men as a group of males is part of the organized craft's defence against the employers.' This sexuality, alienated as it is, is exploited as a means of class solidarity, even though some men feel very uncomfortable about these practices and may indeed welcome women's entry into men's workgroups as a way of changing the culture. However, as with managers' exploitation of sexuality, there is a further complication. For Cockburn adds:

> Many women who have reasons to work with compositors will confirm my experience that they make a big show of apologizing for 'bad language', explaining that in the normal way, as men with men, they are accustomed to use language that would offend women's ears.[17]

Thus men's class solidarity involves the exclusion of women to some degree and also a certain definition by men of what it is to be feminine. Again economic and gender relations are acting upon each other. Such practices, although distinct, may merge into sexual harassment.

Sexual harassment

Sexual harassment occurs at all levels in the workplace, from the shop floor to management. The scale and possibilities of action against harassment are described in a number of British and American texts. The following types of men's behaviour constitute harassment: eyeing up and down; suggestive looks at parts of the body; regular sexual remarks/jokes; unwanted cheek kissing on meeting and parting; asking out on dates despite refusals; unwanted touching or patting; pinching or grabbing; direct sexual proposition; forcible sexual aggression; and the use of pin-ups.

Recent British surveys include those by *Cosmopolitan* magazine, which found 11 per cent of women readers had been subject to persistent, unwanted advances at work;[18] the Liverpool branch of NALGO, which indicated a quarter of women experienced harassment from men in their current workplace, and a half at some time in their working lives;[19] Alfred Marks Bureau, which found that 51 per cent of the women respondents had experienced some form of unwanted sexual response during their working lives;[20] that by Cary Cooper and Marilyn Davidson of women managers, which found that 52 per cent had suffered in this way;[21] another by Camden NALGO which stated that 70 per cent of women had been harassed.[22] The most recent survey that I know of is by TUCRIC, the Leeds trade union resource centre, in which 59 per cent of women from traditional and non-traditional industries had said they experienced harassment frequently.[23] Sexual harassment, although varying in intensity from place to place, or industry to industry, is clearly widespread. Most surveys and critical discussion have tended to focus on the experiences of women rather than why men behave as they do.

Sexual harassment is not about sexual relationships or attempts to attain them. Generally such behaviour is so mindless and impersonal that any but the most hardened are likely to be turned off by it. Sexual harassment by managers and men in positions of authority seems to occur most often in those industries where women are traditionally employed. It cannot be explained as a means of directly exploiting sexuality for economic ends, for if anything it limits the productivity and efficiency of women workers. This suggests that managerial harassment arises from the general level of harassment that operates throughout society and/or other factors particular to the workplace; for example, in the everyday workings of some organizations there is a degree of sexual harassment that appears to be mild, innocent, even friendly. In her study of a Bristol tobacco factory Anna Pollert describes how

> on top of . . . the discipline of work and of factory rules . . . as women, they were exposed to constant sexual patronization, not just from the charge-hands and foremen, but from any men that worked around them: 'Hey, gorgeous', 'Do us a favour, love', 'Come here, sexy' – all are familiar forms of address for most women.[24]

A similar study by Sue Webb of a department store showed how sexual banter and pranks were the language of authority and discipline. She points out that ' . . . when (shop) assistants joined in with manager's jokes, allowed themselves to be petted and flattered and even initiated teasing it was always on the men's terms . . .' In this particular store mild harassment in the form of managers' references to 'his girls' and greetings such as 'How's it going, girls?' were part of everyday life.[25] While the women remain the captive audience of particular men, harassment for the men concerned can be both a way of showing authority and a degree of social involvement – breaching marital discipline, taking risks, being one of the boys. Here harassment expresses the contradictions of authority relations: of superiority, and yet still as one of the employees, still doing his own alienating work of 'management'.

There does remain, however, a distinct economic benefit to some managements. Sexual harassment acts as a system of sex discrimination of women workers, a means of indirectly depressing wage levels and reducing women's work experience below that of male counterparts. For example, the Alfred Marks Bureau survey found that 55 per cent of those sexually harassed changed jobs as a result. This combination of economic and sexual pressure is particularly intense for ethnic minority women, also vulnerable to racial harassment. In certain jobs, such as waitressing, there is pressure from both male customers and managers.

Sexual harassment by men workers appears to occur on an even larger scale than that by managers. The Leeds TUCRIC study found that as compared with traditional women's industries, twice the number of women (96 per cent) employed in journalism, police work, certain manual trades and so on, had experienced harassment. The study also showed that harassment was twice as great; twice as persistent; and generally twice as likely from co-workers than from managers and supervisors. It would seem that the less segregated a workplace the more likely sexual harassment will be.

Sexual harassment can act as a powerful form of economic protection and exclusion from men's territory. Women workers are perceived as a threat to wage levels or to solidarity between men. This may account for high levels of harassment in non-traditional industries; but not the variations in its severity amongst those industries.

Since many of these industries also have dehumanizing work conditions, harassment could be interpreted as a rather pathetic attempt to create some human contact in reaction to this alienation, or as just another alienated act. Social relationships at work are indeed part of that work. Just as 'labour is *external* to the worker, i.e. does not belong to his essential being . . .'[26] so is the sexual harassment of female co-workers.

Finally to complete the picture it is necessary to look at men's ambivalence and even opposition to sexual harassment. A man working in an engineering design office reported on repeated harassment of a woman worker who 'joins in':

> This is very upsetting for me . . . it is degrading, there is no creativity, no spontaneity, no uniqueness in such a relationship. What is more difficult is the way in which group support is required, sought and obtained. If one does not join in the banter and games . . . one is 'dull', 'no fun', 'prudish' . . .

It can take considerable courage for individual men to challenge such practices. This would be aided by collective action. Increasing numbers of trade unions and trade unionists are opposing these practices. These unions tend to be white collar, and based in the public sector, with considerable numbers of women who are often well-educated, and often part of or influenced by the women's movement. Usually these campaigns are led by women. A rather unusual one in a dominantly male organisation is that at Sandwell Direct Labour, Birmingham, involving the TGWU, UCATT and EEPTU. The shop stewards committee decided in 1979 'to go out on site and persuade the mainly male workers that these pictures and pin-ups were degrading and offensive to women'.[27] However, a problem remains in that many men, including many trade unionists, seem to draw a divide between non-physical harassment – whistles, looks, leering – and physical harassment – grabbing, kissing, bottom-pinching. This divide may stem partly from the difficulties women face in bringing direct and immediate action against non-physical forms of harassment, but also from the contradictory reasons for harassment. Physical forms are linked more to men's power over and alienation from women, while non-physical forms are linked to men's relations with each other. The latter may often be for other men's benefit and thus more difficult to challenge.[28]

The importance of non-physical harassment for relations between men is illustrated by that most objectified of forms, pin-ups and calendars. There have been several incidents where someone has used, or threatened to use male nudes alongside or instead of female nudes.[29] In each the reactions have been dramatic, particularly from management. A lone man in a council housing department decided to put up a few pictures of nude men as a protest against increasing numbers of pictures of nude women at work. The response was immediate:

He was accused of being a pervert, it was implied he was a homosexual – the term itself of course being used as a term of abuse – he was not fit to be a Local Government Officer and his work was no good anyway. None of these accusations . . . was true, but the other man did a character assassination of him in front of his supervisor, from whom he was expecting support. Far from being supported he was browbeaten. When this failed he was given a patronizing homily on 'all working together as a happy family', etc. He then challenged his superior to make a statement that all naked pictures should be removed of both men and women; this was refused on the grounds that pictures of women are 'normal' and those of men are not. He was then threatened with dismissal and sensing that at that time not even his union would back

him, he was forced to give in. Some months later he
resigned . . .

Pin-ups are thus not just about the display, harassment and
exploitation of women, but also a statement that men cannot
or should not be treated in this way. To do so is to threaten
the 'solidarity' of men, even of management *and* workers, to
disrupt 'good working relations'.

Horseplay

Horseplay between men is perhaps the least researched
aspect of men's sexuality at work. It consists of intense
physical contact, in the form of 'high-jinks', such as
grabbing of men's genitals from behind, poking fingers up
bottoms, rubbing chests, attacking with brooms, or T-
squares, or simply hearty behaviour with hugging and firm
hand contact, sometimes helped along by alcohol. It may be
accompanied by a verbal culture where men 'affectionately'
refer to each other as 'cunts' or 'tits' or 'old fuckers' but rarely
as 'friends'. As with the sexual expletives of the composing
room and the use of women nudes as pin-ups, this form of
sexual behaviour is primarily for men only. But unlike the
previous two types it is not based on the objectification of
women but rather sexuality between men, perhaps one of
the reasons why it has received so little attention. Horseplay
commonly occurs in army camps, prisons and various
closed institutions. It is less well-documented in factories
and offices.

A typical example of horseplay, in a small chemical
processing plant in Bradford, is led by a small number of
men but indulged in by up to 20 other men out of a total
workforce of about 60 men. Those involved are not seen as
homosexual; they identify as straight, are married with
children, although a few of the leading lights, the mavericks,
speak as if they 'would have anybody of either sex' given the
chance.

So, how do we begin to explain this particular type of

sexual behaviour? First the importance of the physical proximity of workers. These work teams are all male; activity is mainly in men's own teams, although there is some 'cross-fertilization' between teams as most have worked overtime with other teams. It develops between men who already have established some sort of working rapport; newcomers are encouraged to conform. These workers do not have routine access to women workers, and are generally polite to their faces, whilst leering and nudging behind women's backs. Perhaps single sex horseplay is simply the form of sexual behaviour most easily available. However, this doesn't explain why it should occur in this workplace and not others.

Horseplay results from the combination of men's power and men's dehumanizing experiences. Men have power of two sorts here – collective labour power and individual power over individual women as husbands and fathers outside. The way this is expressed concretely is in a macho heterosexual male culture. Power is shown not so much through explicit competition, for that might threaten collective power, as through the continual demonstration of independence. There is a constant flow of humour, repartee and ribaldry about women, marriage, homosexuality. This is generally at a fairly superficial level with reference to men's own marriages maintained in formal, conventional terms. To talk otherwise would be to appear less powerful and more dependent. Men may occasionally offer another emotional support, but only on a once and for all basis. Friendships tend not to be long term. Any sign of emotional or social dependence of one man on another is instead an invitation to take the mickey. Such dependent relationships are seen as more appropriate to a woman in marriage. In this male culture, horseplay, therefore is the physical expression of what is happening socially all the time. For most men in this situation, it is an opportunity to show they can 'give it' and 'take it'. For some it may also be an opportunity to express latent homosexuality but certainly not to come out. For these men, participating in the 'cut and thrust' shows their individual power and their collective powers: they form a male elite.

This is, however, only half the story, for horseplay also seems to derive more directly from the alienating nature of work. In particular it has increased following the introduction of a new technological process with greater mechanization and automation, where there is far less personal responsibility for each man. In the old system jobs were less interchangeable; men worked as a team and had to be aware of how others were getting on; there was even some degree of competition within the team. Men could be independent through the job and so satisfy the requirements of male power. Paradoxically it is now harder to show both independence and social bonding between men; horseplay serves to do both. Men's alienation from the work is expressed in their realization that they are redundant (or almost are) from the work. Horseplay fights back against that feeling of redundancy.

In addition, such men know that they are redundant in another way. Working only with men co-workers, on a continental shift system of days, afternoons, then nights, they are separated from the work of reproduction, the business of caring for others, particularly children. As two men in another chemical company described it: 'This continental really messes my system about: on the day shift I'll eat like a pig, you know, about five meals a day. On nights I don't eat or sleep'. 'I hate the night shift . . . I get awful irritable with the kids. I won't have the telly on if I'm working nights.'[30] Thus horseplay may be a largely unsuccessful attempt to overcome these alienations, to integrate sexuality back into personal relationships.

Men's power and men's alienation

Men's power comes from their status – as husbands and fathers – and from their position in the workplace pecking order. Alienation occurs through technology and the use of labour by big business; from women; and from reproduction. Perhaps above all for men alienation is from each other. Particular forms of power for some men, for example, managers, result in their alienation from workers. The sexual behaviour of many male workers can be seen as both showing solidarity and alienation, as, for example, in the use of sexuality as a talking point.

There is an urgent need to develop a more creative relationship between child care and work which would enhance men's relationships to children and other dependants. Men's relationship to child care is often characterized by exclusion. Many men are either removed from or avoid the work of caring for children and other dependents, yet miss the sensual and emotional contact. They may experience a powerful contradiction between keeping in control and wanting intimate human contact. Increased involvement in caring work can help to resolve this contradiction. This would also be helped by shortening the working week; by giving greater rewards for work with children and for other caring work; by job sharing and flexi-time; by introducing the option of part time work within full time job contracts; and by more immediate arrangements such as workplace nurseries.

There are also more specific changes – necessary within the workplace itself. These entail working in a less alienating environment, where workers are in direct control of their work. This means ending managerial control of workers' movement, particularly women's throughout the workplace. Men concerned to oppose oppressive sexual behaviour have to assist in taking initiatives, both formally, through trade union activity, and informally in everyday conversations with workmates.

This in turn suggests changes in relationships *between men* at work, whereby sexual harassment and exploitation of sexuality are firmly opposed at the same time as we express more honestly to ourselves and each other, our hopes, fears and ambivalences. Simply raising the question of, say, sexual banter for serious discussion with other men can itself be part of this process. Men can give each other mutual support and encouragement in opening up such difficult topics, especially when there may be threats of sanctions from other men. All this can be part of developing an intimacy between men that opposes sexism and reduces both men's power and men's alienation. Such new ways of being with men at work may be risky but promise new forms of solidarity between men and with women, that are not based on false divisions and sexist self-images. If intimacy between men was usual at work there would be no need for sexual harassment and horseplay. So is our sexuality at work really beyond our control?

8. Desire and pregnancy

This chapter is concerned with the ways in which men feel and think about pregnancy. It is not about fatherhood, although the two are obviously linked. It argues that however well men accept and confront the meaning of fatherhood, many of us are still largely incompetent in dealing with the meaning of pregnancy. This chapter will look primarily at the contradictions between the myths which surround pregnant women; the contradictions raised pose a number of thorny problems for men, especially where the relationship between love and sex is concerned.

Such a discussion is clearly a very personal one. Yet it cannot be undertaken solely on the basis of the personal experiences of a few men. Nor can it be undertaken on the basis of a general history of patriarchy, which fails to explain the specific conditions under which men respond to pregnancy and act out their consequent desires. I will, therefore, attempt to outline the historical conditions of male power in relation to pregnancy and fatherhood, and then analyse within this context the specific problems of male responses to pregnancy.

I should emphasize that in putting forward such an argument my main concern is with change: that is, with men's ability to change from a protected position of power over women to one in which the world is shared equally. Without the possibility of such change this book and this chapter would be pointless. Yet change is not an easy matter. It involves re-thinking issues which are subtle, complex, and difficult to confront. What I have to say, therefore, is a contribution to rethinking.

I have inevitably left gaps and avoided issues which others

will consider important. I have, for example, been unable to take into detailed account the experiences of men whose background is *not* European. Similarly I have made no distinctions on the basis of class – not because I think there are none, but because proper enumeration of them is beyond my expertise. This is, then, a very personal view.

Yet having said that, I should also add that my experience may well be shared with others. It may be an experience touched with bitterness, pain and confusion. Only our particular, personal histories can explain in what ways we feel similarly, or differently, to others.

Male power

There are many reasons why men want to have children, or at least think they want them. In the general historical sense, fatherhood is a public statement of private power which in turn invests the father with a status among men. Through fatherhood, men occupy the sanctified territory of family responsibility. Within the Judeo–Christian world view fatherhood is the justification of sexual desire.

Such a world view sees the legitimate form of fatherhood as biological. Step-fathers, though to a lesser extent than step-mothers, often experience distance between themselves and their children. Adoption is rarely seen as a first choice. There is an assumption that the ability to 'sire' children is an essential factor in being a man. Male sexuality has traditionally been divorced from the familial, nurturing and child-bound context which is seen as part of women's sexuality. Yet it is through the 'potency' which is demonstrated in being a father that many men gain their power, particularly over other men.

Since the beginning of industrial capitalism there has been an intimate connection between gender division and the organization of production. There occurred a separation between women and men as consequence of the male domination of the public world of labour, the professions, and the state. Women were relegated to the private sphere of the home where they were supposed to bring up children. Women were also expected to cater for the sexual needs of their husbands without reference to their own desire. Where women, and sometimes children, were brought into the workforce it was at the lowest level and with maximum expendability. In addition to such work, women were also expected to perform their 'proper' role as wife, mother and family caretaker. As a general description this is surely true of the nineteenth century in which competitive or laissez-faire capitalism held sway and workforces remained small and compartmentalized.[1] Family and often town or village life was centred around a particular industry or even a single firm.

During the twentieth century, with the development of large corporations and multinationals, and the ensuing technological revolution, there have been significant changes in the ways in which people work. Increasing unemployment, the replacement of the male industrial working class by machinery, the extensive use of women in industries such as catering, and the extensive refinement of computerized management, have reduced the importance and power of men as family 'breadwinners' and industrial producers.

A hundred years ago it was assumed that men, as husbands and fathers, should undertake full economic responsibility for their wives and children. The law was geared to ensuring that the family was in every sense the private property of the man. Although women were expected to help 'refine' their men out of work hours, the church vested in men the responsibility for the moral welfare of their wives and children. Social disapproval or legal punishment would be the result only of serious neglect or abuse. Moreover, just as women were expected to become wives and mothers, men were expected to become husbands and fathers. Various instruments of the state or large private and charitable institutions including the medical and legal professions, have replaced male autonomy and control with increasingly technological and sophisticated forms of corporate and state control.

There has been a widespread re-assertion of the idealized values of the self-reliant man and his family, in which women are the ministering angels overseeing the upbringing of the lawyers, doctors, computer technicians and military heroes of the future. The medical profession has already increased its control in family areas. It is not only reproduction in all its stages which is watched over hawkishly and determined morally and physically by doctors, but birth control and abortion as well.

Such a history suggests that men want children in order to fulfil a role within a society where their power has undergone a considerable transformation. Yet at a personal level men want children for more complicated reasons. Children provide one of the few opportunities in life, perhaps the only one, for some men to be intimate, tender and loving without fearing a consequent loss of masculinity.

Perhaps as a consequence of the dispossession of male power, together with the increasing demands of the women's movement, there is a growing male preoccupation with children – children not simply as evidence of their manhood or as heirs to their name, but as objects of love and care. In the last few years the appearance of Hollywood films like *Kramer Versus Kramer* and *Ordinary People* has reflected a growing desire by men to re-establish bonds with their children. However, such films are reactionary in their tendency to establish these bonds by a progressive exclusion of the woman from her central role as parent.

Such a development is full of confusion. I share with a number of men I know a desire not just to be a father, but to be a father on an equal footing with the mother. I suspect, though I don't know, that such a desire is increasing. Yet, quite distinct from this, there is also a group of men, acting quite openly in response to the women's movement, whose stated aim of 'men's liberation' is aimed at restoring the father's custody over children in the case of break-up or divorce.[2] Their battle appears, appropriately, to be centred in the legal and professional sphere, a reflection of the class status of the men themselves. Its driving impulse appears to be a clawing back of the power they have lost to women through the emergence of feminism.

Where men do express a genuine desire to be fathers, their position is perhaps more complex. There is still an impulse to regard biological fatherhood as the ideal. Yet it would be dishonest to argue that this is the only reason. My experience, and that of some men and women I know, suggests that even if legal and social barriers were removed, there is still a psychological and emotional distance between the non-biological parent and child, and a suspicion that the relationship is somehow incomplete.

Fetishism

Little of the growing literature in which men seek to outline the historical path to the present, directly tackles the issues of male response to reproduction. In most cases where fatherhood is discussed, the mother is absent, or remains only as an abstract emblem or fiction in the background. A good example is the article on fatherhood in an otherwise pioneering American book about men's responses to the women's movement, *Men and Masculinity*. In his article, Michael Silverstein makes a tiredly ironic attempt at self-criticism, in which occurs the longest of his two references to the mother of his children: 'Even an academician has to get himself at least one woman and a child or two.'[3]

We might expect advances to have been made in the ten years since this book was published. I am not aware of them, although the attention given by feminists and the press to contraception has engendered something, at least, in the way of discussion of the relationship between desire and reproduction. Yet the confusion certainly hasn't cleared. We need to address this confusion with as little sentimentality as possible. To do so, we need to confront the way in which men continue to separate sex from its reproductive, emotional and social contexts.

While the problem of fatherhood may begin in early childhood (and I shall return to this later), it becomes a conscious reality when we first ejaculate, and make the important connection between ejaculation and pleasure. While we have experienced our bodies as sexual before this, the experience has rarely been associated with reproduction. It is only when, through some form of sex education or through a haphazard putting together of the pieces that come to us through experience, that we make the connection.

Since the penis has been invested with a controlling power in sexual relationships between women and men, the ability to fertilize has been elevated into a myth of male abundance. Our potential as fathers has been named 'virility'. This name has come to represent a power which is social and psychological and which hides the realities of the penis itself in a web of mystery and threat. One way in which this mystery is sustained is through the transformation, within the dominant culture, of the penis into the phallus. Taken by itself the penis is a floppy appendage which rises and falls and is the source of a number of pleasures. The phallus is more than this. It is the physical organ represented as continuously erect; it is the abundance and inexhaustability of male desire; it is a dominant element within our culture.

The way in which, as men, we collude in the myths which sustain these names is, at least in part, brought about by a fetishism which turns not only women, but our own sexualities, into commodites. We progressively reduce ourselves, and others, to specific physical parts which are then separated and isolated from the whole. We become our penises; women become breasts and vaginas; and the rest slips out of focus. In the interests of capital, we become part of the range of products which are advertised and hawked round the market place. Advertising for cigarettes, alcohol, fast cars and other commodities use sexuality to sell us back to ourselves in fragmented form. Desirability as men, virility as an expression of being men, the ownership of women and children – these are sold as a package in which we are the central item.

Men are preoccupied with their penises. This is not only because the penis causes the most intense sensuous pleasure, but because this pleasure is inseparable from ejaculation. The production of semen is one of the crucial concrete symbols of masculinity. But it is not only the fact of this production, it is the quantity and nature of it that is important. Much explicit pornography focuses on the semen itself: its colour, quantity, temperature, viscosity, and the distance it can be ejaculated. Male writers as far apart as Lawrence, Genet, Roth and Fowles have displayed an equal preoccupation with semen.

What is significant is the way in which semen has been separated, both in the representation of sexuality and in sexual activity itself, from its emotional and procreative meanings. In pornography, the semen is ejaculated, not into but onto women, and as we see it on the screen is totally divorced from the woman herself. The assumption is that for the man to ejaculate inside the woman the pleasurable dimension of what is being represented would be lost, both through the invisibility of the concrete symbol of power, and through the association that it would have with conception.

It has been one of the gains of feminism that women have managed to distinguish between the pursuit of pleasure through sex, and the pursuit of motherhood. Men, however, have always acted as though such a distinction, between sex and reproduction, were a natural part of our sexuality. Our sexuality is narcissistic – a preoccupation with the penis and ejaculation. We are ourselves both the subject and the object of pleasure. The woman remains, for heterosexual men, a medium through which this pleasure is achieved. The reality, for her, of conception and pregnancy is denied by men. A remarkable contradiction for men is that, while the very power of the semen to fertilize is part of what creates the narcissism in male sexuality, that power is isolated through this narcissism, from the reality of conception.

Male fetishism is bound up with men's confusion in the face of women's experience of reproduction. Unable to understand what is going on, unable to relate to the entire emotional and social context of our sexual activity the way women are forced to, we reduce ourselves to fragments, abdicate our responsibilities, and build fears and threats for ourselves and for the women in our relationships.

The take-over by men

At the heart of this confusion is the contradiction between the separation of men's desire and reproduction, and men's tendency to regard pregnancy and childbirth as the fulfilment not only of their social role as father, but of their sexual 'potency' as well. This fulfilment of potency can be recognized, for example, in the pride with which men refer to their children. I recall a typical statement made by a man of fifty just after the birth of his fourth child: 'Well,' he said 'at least it shows I can still get it up.'

Such a self-regarding response to pregnancy and childbirth is only one part of the paradox. The other is the way in which some men regard pregnant women and mothers, generally and specifically. In its crudest form, this response can be seen in street commentary. When a pregnant woman walks past, she is sometimes accompanied, and indeed assaulted, by knowing nudges and laughter, or by a statement such as 'we know what *you've* been doing'. There is a sense of men disowning their embarassment and unease. Underneath this may be a deeper sense that pregnancy confirms a now absent male desire. As such, it represents the 'fact' and consequence of penetration and possession of woman by man and thus becomes the *end* of desire itself. In the most extreme form of this representation, pregnancy is a public saturation of sexual energy, a visible collar indicating the completeness of possession. On the other hand, in some men's eyes pregnancy may be a confirmation of the woman's continued sexuality, even of her promiscuity. Pregnancy is a seen as a public punishment for having stepped outside the accepted social context in which her sexuality is supposed to be anchored.

It is paradoxically consistent with these responses that

some men are unable to find a pregnant woman desirable. It is only partly the case that this is an outcome of the visible proof that she is 'private property', and therefore out of bounds to other men. It is also part of the important process in which men try to deny the sexuality of the pregnant woman. There is considerable evidence that this 'desexualization', is widespread in Western culture. A highly significant indication is that while there is still a taboo, deriving particularly from the nineteenth century, against breast-feeding in public, it is nevertheless possible to represent women who are breast-feeding with no expectation that their breasts will be the object of erotic desire.[4]

Another indication is a common experience borne out by many of the women and men I have spoken to, that of the breakdown of the relationship or marriage during pregnancy. Both in conversation and in written interviews, women have referred to the waning desire of their lovers or husbands, and of the man's changing perceptions of her, during pregnancy. In an interview quoted by Anne Oakley, for example, Jane Tarrent expresses this very clearly: 'I think he looks at me in a different way . . . I don't suppose he finds me so sexy . . . he thinks of me more as the mother of his child.'[5]

Some women also remarked, in conversation, that they too experienced a waning of desire after about five or six months of pregnancy, and that the primary relationship was with the growing child and their own bodies. Among the women I spoke to these were, however, in the minority, and for most there was at least some desire toward their lovers or husbands. Men have supported this evidence. There appears to be a pattern in which many men experienced their first 'affair' when their partners were entering the final stages of pregnancy.

Sexuality and pregnancy

The theological and medical appropriation of women's

bodies has had profound implications for both women and men. The significance of the development has been demonstrated in a growing body of research generated by Michel Foucault in his *Introduction to the History of Sexuality*. Foucault argues that the situation arises from the process in which women's sexualities are constructed by dominant cultural and social discourses. These sexualities are all determined to some extent by the woman's relationship to the family, either within or outside it. His argument is summarised clearly by Kathy Myers.

> For Foucault, power works to produce a multiplicity of female sexualities which work to maintain the social order: eg, the production of the ideology of 'romance', of 'hysteria', the 'nervous woman', 'frigid wife' or insatiable 'nymphomaniac'. Certain forms of female sexuality support the family structure, others are outlawed from it: eg, pornography, prostitution and lesbianism. For Foucault this public/private dichotomy, far from challenging the social order, works to secure and legitimate the parameters of acceptable and unacceptable behaviour.[6]

Within this range of sexualities pregnancy is omitted, partly because Foucault does not recognize the possibility of there being a sexuality of pregnancy itself; and partly because within the history he traces pregnancy was part of those areas of women's matrimonial, and therefore legitimate, duty in which the economy of sexual pleasure did not figure. He refers, therefore, to those 'dangerous periods of pregnancy or breastfeeding, forbidden times of Lent or Abstinence',[7] when desire was seen as wholly inappropriate. He does not mention menstruation in this context, another area associated with women's reproductive capacity, in which desire has been traditionally denied.

Foucault argues that the removal of pregnancy from the domain of women's sexualities was a function of the process which he calls 'hysterization', that is, a process assumed to be 'saturated with sexuality' in which women's bodies are subjected to medical control.[8] Pregnant women are relegated to the family in which they exist solely for their forthcoming or existing children. This subjection to the sphere of medical practices involved an assumption shared by men, and colluded in by women, that pregnancy was a recognizable pathological condition. This involved treating women as somehow afflicted and requiring treatment. Pregnancy is still treated as part of pathological science – obstetrics. One of the effects of this has been to deny the right of women themselves to determine the process of pregnancy and childbirth. Another effect has been the male tendency to respond to pregnancy as one might respond, for example, to cancer or madness.

What makes the ideology of such a classification so powerful and so persevering is the way in which it has also been imbued, both within catholic and protestant traditions, with a sacred purpose. The married woman's pregnant body has become the speaking image of an ideal, the 'font of life'. This body is seen as removed from desire or sexual expectation. Simone de Beauvoir describes this tradition:

> her bosom, which was previously an erotic figure, can now be freely shown, for it is a source of life; even religious pictures show us the Virgin Mother exposing her breast as she beseeches her son to save Mankind. With her ego surrendered, alienated in her body and in her social dignity the mother enjoys the comforting illusion of feeling that she is a human being, *in herself a value*.[9]

The woman is, therefore, fulfilling for men and for the dominant culture a mystery and alchemy which is partly her own, partly the possession of society as a whole. She is said to live beyond the domain in which sexual touch has any meaning. She is engaged in a ritual which men feel to be her own, and from which therefore we absent ourselves. We construct a myth in which the woman, through her pregnancy, is fulfilling herself *as* a woman.

The threat of pregnancy

The apparent ritual in which the pregnant woman is involved is both an excuse for men to persevere in illusion, and a source of the threat, pain, jealousy or envy which frequently mark the male experience of pregnancy and early fatherhood.

Envy is grounded in a traditonal expression of the difference between the 'cultural' and the 'natural'. Women are classed as 'naturally' creative – their creativity is the ability to conceive and bear children. This belief frequently comes across as an assumption that pregnancy and childbearing are the domain within which women fulfil themselves as women. Yet it also entails the belief that men, because they are incapable of such a natural act of creation, are forced to create artificially, thus producing what we call culture. The relationship which then emerges between women as natural and men as cultural producers is one in which envy has taken hold. Most men appear to feel considerable unease about the ability of women to create a recognizable, complex and growing being within their own bodies. For men, such an intricate partnership with the object of creative activity is impossible.

There is a considerable body of creative work which is the best evidence available for this male unease and envy, often expressed as aggression. In the work of the French poet and dramatist Artaud (originator of the Theatre of Cruelty), cultural creation is an attempt to imitate, or re-enact, the process of being born. The poem or play therefore becomes something of a substitute for procreative activity. A poet I know claims that his work is no more than an attempt to emulate the process of giving birth. Yet in the face of what he sees as the 'ultimate' creativity to which women have sole access, his work is an inadequate and poor relation. It is interesting in this light that throughout its history poetry has been self-regarding, concerned with the process itself by which the poem comes into being. In the work of Shakespeare, Donne, the Romantics, and Yeats – for example – there are many instances in which the birth of a child is the ideal against which the birth of a poem is measured.[10]

What is indicated in this cultural history is a male fear of the power women have to give birth, and perhaps a fear of birth itself. If it is not fear, then it is certainly envy, however indirectly that envy may be felt or expressed. While I acknowledge the force of such envy or fear, I do not believe that men can be reduced simply to this. The argument made by Mary Daly and Phyllis Chessler, amongst others, that men are defined by the absence of a womb and motivated by envy of women, seems to me simplistic, claiming as a total motivation something which is rather a source of unease.[11]

A second, related, envy arises from the apparent exclusivity of pregnancy and birth which emphasizes and highlights the fact of difference between men and women. The woman herself, and those parts of her body which the man once felt to be his own terrain, have become public in a way which is not simply an affirmation to the world of his virility and her fertility, but is also *self-absorbed*. The woman attracts attention in her own right not as the man's wife or lover, and not because she displays a 'sexiness' which he hoards as his property. During pregnancy, the woman becomes interesting to herself, to members of her family, and to other women not only for what she is experiencing now, but for what she is about to experience. And the sharing of those experiences has historically been a realm exclusively enjoyed by women.

Men find themselves excluded by a shared language and imagery which we do not understand because we have belittled and berated it. The relationship with women no longer has the direct power we have been accustomed to and come to expect. We stand on one side of a veil of mystery which we ourselves have helped to construct. When the child is finally born and absorbs the mother's time and energy men are made, at least temporarily, irrelevant.

This exclusivity is perhaps stronger for men than it might be for women were the situation reversed. There is a tendency among some men to narrow the focus, over time, of their emotional energy and demands. Where women tend to spread their emotional needs more evenly among women friends, heterosexual men deny the emotional dimension of their relationships with other men, and concentrate their demands on one woman (two if we include the mother). Thus the shock to the emotional system is perhaps greater for men because in the exclusivity of pregnancy the one source of emotional supply is cut off.[12]

There are several dimensions to the exclusion of men during pregnancy and early motherhood. One involves the progressive de-eroticization of the relationship during pregnancy. Another involves the reality that women *do* act out a self-contained drama in which men have no part, between themselves and their own bodies, and between themselves and the child growing inside them. In this sense, the exclusion is no different from that which results from friendships between women, or between women and male friends or other lovers. What gives the exclusion of pregnancy its particular power, however, is that in pregnancy the man feels that the women carries the man's social investment, the product of his masculinity.

Men deny rather than accept or explore their relationships with their bodies. In order for the male self-image to be complete – in the experience of heterosexual men, that is – it needs to be identified with that of a sexual other, usually a woman. The proof that our image is complete is the pregnancy of the woman. She is, in these terms, the terrain in which our sperm is invested rather as though it were money on a stock-market. We are, however, emotionally slow to understand what is going on *for* the woman when she becomes pregnant. It rises ahead of us as a threat carried in her shape and her physical as well as emotional experiences of the changes she is undergoing.

The depth of this experience for men should not be underrated. It is not surprising that the drama of pregnancy is, and represents, a challenge to the man's position in the relationship. While some men may reject the sexuality of the woman, they themselves feel, often with some justice, that their sexuality too has been rejected. It is also possible that the intensity of the woman's relationship with her pregnant body and then with the child, raises the possibility for men that their importance for the woman has been reduced to little more than their ability to fertilize.

It is not of course inevitable that men are so excluded. Historically, we are profoundly responsible for the position we find ourselves in. The male tendency to withdraw emotionally from women, and to predicate her sexuality on our own fears, creates a great distance between us and the experience we are observing but taking little or no part in. And to underline this difference we have reified, and treated as natural and ordained, the differences existing between men and women, particularly in the sphere of reproduction.

Yet it is only partly on our fears that we predicate the sexuality of women. Related to this, and equally important, is the history of the production of 'desirability', or sexual attractiveness, through representation. The image of slenderness and sexiness, often related to clothing, which dominates representations of women in western media and art histories, lives in sharp contrast to the reality of most women, including pregnant women.

For many men the media images of women have taken on a more powerful reality than women themselves. Images in advertising, on the screen, in pornography, are a result of male fantasy. Yet at the same time they direct the development of fantasy and provide the model by which men judge their own experience or failures of experience. Fantasy in this sense is predominantly sexual, the woman's body inviting men to take their pleasure in it.

It has become virtually impossible to represent the pregnant woman as sexual, or as an object of erotic desire, except perhaps in rare cases where pregnancy is fetishized as an object of pornography.[13] The pregnant woman represents saturation or the end of desire. Therefore the visible shape of the pregnancy prohibits an opposite erotic representation.

Often it is when sight and touch are brought together that fantasy meets reality. It may be the expectation, anticipation or memory of touch rather than touch itself. With it come meanings. As Roland Barthes enumerates in his book *A Lover's Discourse*:

> A squeeze of the hand . . . a tiny gesture within the palm, a knee which doesn't move away, an arm extended, as if quite naturally, along the back of a sofa and against which the other's head gradually comes to rest – this is the paradisiac realm of subtle and clandestine signs: a kind of festival not of sense but of meaning.[14]

These meanings, created through the form and sensuous presence of pregnancy, contain both the social and psychological means by which the erotic is prohibited. It is also, paradoxically, the route through which the erotic might be restored. It may well be that for many women the absence of male desire during pregnancy is a relief. Yet in heterosexual relationships where both the pregnancy and the eroticism are potentially sources of intimacy and pleasure, this cannot in the long run be welcome. It is important to restore at least the possibilities of eroticism: partly as a way of regaining lost or floundering intimacy; partly as a way of breaking anachronistic prohibitions. It is also through an eroticism which is determined by intimacy and knowledge of itself, rather than by representation, that men can discover more intimately what is involved not only in a 'festival of meaning' but in the reality of their relationships.

I am arguing here, that a restoration of the erotic during pregnancy is important. But I am not interested in merely extending the range of sexualities in which men can find pleasure. It is because pregnancy has caused so many problems for the relationship between a man and a pregnant woman that I am on the lookout for ways of breaking the pattern. And the domain in which the erotic lives contains, at once, the most powerful prohibitions, and the most powerful way through them.

Prohibitive as it has been, however, this history I refer to has thrown up many glosses on the problem. In art history the pregnant woman has been a source of sensual desire, and of models for the church. In the work of Michelangelo the sequence of conception, pregnancy and birth has provided both the sensuous immediacy of his work and the paradoxical statement of moral control. And in the painter Bellini, another man of the Renaissance, there is a powerful contradiction between the image of mother as virgin, and her sensuous existence at the threshold where, as Julia Kristeva has argued, culture meets nature.[15] Poetry, as I have already discussed, contains the same mischievious paradoxes.

The possibilities to which Barthes and Kristeva, through her analysis of Bellini, refer are those in which pregnancy can be seen as containing its own dramatic form. Drama is the narrative in which the moral, political, social and personal world meet under extreme tension. In pregnancy the drama is wrested from the scope of male privilege. It is played out between the woman and her child, her body, her coterie of friends. It is immediate and sensuous. For men, this is a difficult drama to experience because there is no audience participation of the kind we would like or are used to.

We find it hard to be placed in such a drama, hard to resume the control which until these moments we have so freely wielded. Fantasy and image disappear because they have no place, are contradicted by the overpowering reality of what is going on in there. And furthermore, the child inside the woman is becoming real (our son, our daughter), and has formed a relationship with the mother. Intervention is impossible. We are powerless.

In recognizing and responding to this drama we as men have missed one of its primary significances: its potential for participation, for us to create a role other than the one we have taken so far. We are capable, through actions which might well challenge others' perception of our masculinity, of becoming caretakers to this drama, of helping it along. For most of us the impulse is to depart, to clear out of the audience and find elsewhere the assurance we need that we are men, powerful, lovable, and still in control.

The child is father to the man

Yet these analyses are in the end too simple. Men are more complex, more contradictory than I have been giving them credit for. Men's traditional withdrawal from the process of reproduction is lodged at a deeper level than can be dealt with, by the man himself, at the time when the problem arises. This deeper level involves the development of male sexuality, and responses to women, during the early years of infancy. In consequence, the male response to pregnancy seems to involve a re-enactment of the terrors as well as the pleasures surrounding our relationships with our own mothers and with the process of birth itself. Although I can only outline the issues I am convinced that the gaps in our analyses and understanding can only be filled if we address the problems associated with the development of infantile sexuality and its repercussions for the adult male. Revolving around the initial Oedipal conflict, and the subsequent removal of the mother as object of sexual desire, infantile sexuality is crucial to our response to the pregnancy of our sexual partner.

While the materialist account of male sexuality – grounded in the will to grasp power – is persuasive, it does not account for the long history of men's sexual rejection of their pregnant partners. Nor can it explain, except superficially, why men respond as they do. It is becoming clearer that the role of the unconscious is of primary importance. Otherwise, why would men who have stressed the importance of issues like child care, support for their partners, and commitment, still behave as though those recognitions never existed? What is it, we must ask, that drives us in ways we cannot control by listening, reading and deducing? We *know* the commitment and care we should give to our pregnant partners, who are clearly at their most vulnerable. Yet is it still possible for us to deceive, abandon and humiliate them. It is also the case that we deceive and humiliate ourselves.

We may reject psychoanalysis for ourselves. But we

cannot reject the insights which it has unearthed into the way we behave in certain known circumstances. The male response to pregnancy has not been part of the psychoanalytic project. It should be, since it would help to illuminate the repetitive nature of our responses to this among other situations.

In the construction of the Oedipus complex – in which a boy at an early age, tackles the differences between mother and father and finds a place for himself in the relationship with them – the boy begins to identify physically with the father. They both have penises which are different from what the boy has observed about the mother. In the process of this identification, the boy sides with the father and rejects the mother with whom he has had an intense and sensuous relationship. In siding with the father, the boy is also conscious, at least emotionally, that he is duelling with his father for his mother's attention.

In rejecting the mother, the boy is also rejected by her. The process is both mutual and messy. Rejection on both sides creates an unresolved lack in the boy which, at one level, produces an unfulfillable yearning or desire for some re-instatement of the mother's position in the boy's life; and at another level the mother's rejection of the boy becomes imprinted in the memory of this early relationship and lasts throughout the boy's life. Some theorists argue that the damage done by rejection and loss, in this context, is irreparable. I prefer to think that through our relationships with significant other people, there is the capacity for resolution. Central, therefore, to the boy's memory, is the experience of pain, anguish, rejection and loss. It is this centrality which helps to determine one important level in the development of male sexuality. In the relationship with the mother, pleasure is also a clear and unmediated component. It is pleasure which has been denied through the history of repression and prohibition. It is also this pleasure which holds promise for a future rekindling of the erotic in our relationship with pregnancy.

When a man's partner becomes pregnant, the dimension

of this Oedipal conflict is one of which the memory involves loss and pain. Pleasure is taken away from it. We begin to associate our pregnant partner with the rejecting mother. We begin to associate the process of pregnancy and childbirth with our own experiences of being born into a self-contained and pleasurable world which we are then forced to deny. A vicious circle is then set in motion. This includes, perhaps, a further haze of memories including our experience of rivalry and jealousy if our mother became pregnant with another child.

Pregnancy, then, re-activates the memory of rejection. In light of this, we may in turn reject not only the sexuality of our partner and her potential motherhood, but her being, herself as a person. We withdraw from her in case we are once again rejected. When the rejection becomes real, as it frequently does for men, pain is confirmed and loss becomes the central episode of our lives.

It is a pattern which has frequently been observed that in withdrawing from, and hence rejecting our partner, men turn to someone else. In turning to another, our memory of early pain has been resolved. Our position is restored through a re-affirmation of our maleness – a capacity to separate sex from its emotional and social contexts. The other woman becomes, for us, sexuality itself – as though sexuality were separable from everything else – and thereby detached in all senses from the painful relationship with the mother and the pregnant partner. Within this new relationship the man is able, at least for a while, to shed responsibility and concentrate on the pursuit of sensual pleasure, to re-establish the unmediated pleasure he associates with infancy. Caught between fields of infant and adult sexuality, the man forgets his relationships both with the mother whose rejection he has endured because there was no other possibility, and with his partner, whose dramatic and consuming experience is too closely bound up with those early experiences.

Reproduction is an area in which men frequently flounder in relationships with women. The temptation to withdraw in the face of exclusivity and the realm of emotions and memories which underscore it, is irresistable for many men. Withdrawal is, in this context as well as others, a function of the Anglo-Saxon male difficulty in articulating or demonstrating feeling. Yet reproduction holds out a number of silent promises for the relationships between women and men, not least the possibility of the man's caring and loving in response to the woman's needs.

Yet many men reject this possibility as well as rejecting a real but threatening eroticism in their relationship. In doing so, we do considerable damage to women. Yet we also do a considerable damage to ourselves. It seems to me possible for men to resolves the dilemmas held out during pregnancy, and in so doing create some of the conditions by which our sexuality might mature out of its infancy.

9. Fear and Intimacy

A beginning: needing others

I was brought up to denounce whatever fear I was feeling. That I learnt to deny fear meant a refusal to recognize its continuing existence in my life. As I was brought up in a Jewish family who had escaped from Europe only moments before Hitler's concentration camps were to become a cruel and barbarous reality, fear was never far from the surface of my life. I learnt to avoid the horror so as not to be overwhelmed by it. I am only beginning to be able to think about some of this 38 years later, and still find it impossible to accept the reality of what happened to so many in my family. At some level I felt deeply ashamed about what happened, as if I was somehow responsible. I learnt not to show my fear to others as I learnt to hide it from myself. But also I discovered that in hiding my fear I hid my vulnerability. I learnt to listen to others, but not to really share myself.

I had to slowly learn that in blocking my fear I was hurting my capacity for close and loving relationships. Somehow I had to learn to question the image that I was presenting to myself of an easy and happy childhood and begin to work with some of my painful realities. Admitting I needed the help of others was an important step since it questioned the independence and self-sufficiency I inherited with my masculinity. But it was a difficult step since I still thought that therapy was for sick people. This was in 1972 when the left still found it difficult to accept the idea of consciousness raising for men, let alone therapy. I long had the intellectual understandings of Freud, even Reich, but this was different from activity involving myself in a therapeutic practice. I had learnt to use my language and understanding as a way of controlling my experience and relationships. I sensed a crucial difference between talking about feelings and actually experiencing them, though I didn't connect this to the ways that language is used to sustain a particular form of masculine identity. I remember being haunted by a pervasive sense of the 'unreality' of my experience which seemed to be part of the affluent atmosphere of the times. With 1968 politics was to be grounded in an exploration of a shared experience in the emerging black, women's and gay movements.

The connections with therapy were slower to emerge. Laing's work was crucially important in giving this a voice[1], and was part of the impetus in the setting up of Red Therapy, a group that sought to bring therapy and politics into closer relationship with each other.[2] We were open to the insights of psychoanalysis but also felt the significance of the breaks with the Freudian patriarchial and intellectualist tradition being made in what was loosely called the 'growth movement'.[3] We sought to re-appropriate ways of working with somatic and emotional experience while challenging individualism and blindness to the relationships of power and subordination. The focus upon the *quality* of present lived experience and the choices people can make is an important aspect of expressive therapies that needs to be reasserted. It helps question the strength of moralism in the left and the naive assumptions we inherit about personal and social change. Expressive therapies contain an implicit critique of Lacan's intellectualist focus upon language, in a period when many people have returned to traditional forms of psychoanalysis. This is not to set up a false choice between psychoanalysis and other forms of human psychology since people may well need different ways of working at different times in their lives. But it is to open a discussion about the philosophical and political assumptions of different forms of therapy and to question the structuralist terms in which the relationship of psychoanalysis to both feminism and marxism is usually set.

We at least need to be aware of the traditions of criticism of traditional psychoanalytic practice that Reich, Jung and others made, and of the sources for Freud's own break with clinical work, if we aren't to be trapped in Lacan's intellectualist appropriation of Freud through his idea that the unconscious is structured as a language. This is especially important if we wish to sustain the centrality of sexuality and sexual experience in our lives, rather than present sexuality somewhat in the spirit of Foucault's *A History of Sexuality*, as a form of conceptual construction in which anything goes.[4] This also requires a critique of the homophobia and genital orientation found in Reich, while valuing his recognition that individuals themselves, rather than detached therapists, have to recognize the meaning of interpretations and so be the source of qualitative distinctions in the therapeutic process.

This is a difficult path which challenges the traditional power and the silent authority of the analyst, but it is made easier in the context of consciousness raising, which validates and confirms the importance of personal experience. Although it may be easier in the context of group therapy, people often need to work through a transference at a depth and intensity only really available within individual therapy. Again it is important not to be trapped into traditional moralizing that declares certain forms of relationships and sexual experiences as 'right' or 'wrong'. The left has been too crude in its discussion of moral traditions, so that we often find ourselves articulating and living out moral notions we have long broken with intellectually. I've tried to shift the discussion to think more in terms of the *quality* of our relationships and sexual experience.

Sexual politics has helped us transcend an inherited disjunction between accounts of personal experience and notions of social theory and philosophy. We tend to see accounts of personal experiences as examples of general theory. This has helped us to accept the idea that social theory has to be difficult and abstract. Gramsci's *Prison*

Notebooks challenge this pervasive assumption.[5] On the other hand the use of 'we' in this piece can be confusing since it can easily lead me to generalize from a particular experience without being clear enough about its social and historical specificity, and most obviously perhaps, its heterosexist assumptions. I try to be aware of this, though; in discussing notions of fear and intimacy I'm purposefully calling for a different, less detached and more involved relationship with a reader. This has to show itself in the character of the writing. It is part of a process of creating a different politics and sensibility; an opening out of the points at which men might recognize themselves. I think this is more familiar in feminist writing, though the challenge such writing makes to our inherited masculine rationalist traditions of thought and feeling has been rarely explored. This can no longer be taken for granted as a shared generational assumption but has to be part of an intellectual practice to illuminate the notion that 'the personal is political'.

Modern social theory often leaves us with a set of intellectual categories we are to use to order or 'constitute' our experience. This is a deep assumption of structuralist thought that has almost become part of the 'common sense' of intellectual work, though it is deeply at odds with Marx's central insights into the relationship of social consciousness to social being. In truth it has more to do with the continuing influence of a rationalist tradition in France than anything to do with Marx. It is also at odds with the practice of conciousness raising, though it is the way this experience has often been theorized. It tends to render the very category of 'experience' as an intellectual construct — no longer something we can use to decide between different theoretical traditions.

We are trapped into thinking that talk of experience has to be empiricist and we assume that experience exists independently and prior to our understanding. Gramsci makes clear that our common sense speaks out of a particular historical and social experience, though we may be largely unaware of this. What is at issue is the *significance* we give to a particular event or experience; often we have not realised the theoretical significance or importance of what has happened to us. It is central to the practice of consciousness raising that people *rework* their experience, coming to grasp the significance of gender identity in the ways we are treated by others and in the way we come to think and feel about ourselves. This is an integral part of a process of social and historical understanding in which one's individual experience becomes grasped as a shared gender experience. A similar process can happen in the context of therapy, in which people come to experience the significance of a situation or relationship they had taken for granted. This has been a deep flaw with structuralist accounts of psychoanalysis which aren't based upon an experience of a therapeutic process.

Within feminist work the categories of subordination, oppression and objectification are personally experienced by individual women; they are also the source of a deep critique of relations of power in society as a whole. It is because these also operate as social and political categories that it becomes clear how the private and the public are to be brought into relation with each other. This is less clear in exploring masculinity as a social and historical experience. The disdain for the personal and the stance of invulnerability has made masculinity a mystifying experience for men themselves. Heterosexual masculinity sets an impersonal standard which presents itself as 'reality', rather than the specific historical experience of men.

Freud showed that men's behaviour is not guided by the light of impersonal reason. He made us aware that we are vulnerable creatures who can be deeply hurt in our personal relations, though we do everything to flee this knowledge of ourselves. At some level Freud challenges the modern identification of masculinity with reason and science that was firmly established in the seventeenth century Scientific Revolution with all the brutality and cruelty of the witch trials.[6] Freud did not challenge the control that reason exercises over our emotional and somatic lives. He simply gave us a way of facing more of our fear and vulnerability, while also appreciating how hard this personal knowledge is for us to assimilate. It was Reich who showed that the *estrangement* from our experience as men is written into the very experience of our bodies as machines. He knew how much tension and emotion we hold tight in the very organization of our bodies and how easy it is to intellectualize our experience as a defence. He recognized that we have to develop fuller contact with our bodies if we are to develop more responsibility for ourselves as sexual beings.

The significance of notions of fear and vulnerability will have to be *discovered* through a shared experience of masculinity. Most learning helps us to grasp what we have only dimly discerned to be significant and important. The fear of the personal has such broad cultural support that it is difficult to acknowledge the reality of our feelings and how stuck for language and understanding we really are. This means being ready to take the risk of starting an emotional and historical exploration from where we are; I hope I have been able to do this myself.

Vulnerability, sexuality and male identity

As boys, we learn constantly to prove our masculinity. We can never take it for granted. This builds enormous tension into contemporary conceptions of masculinity. Fear is defined as an unacceptable emotion. But in disowning our fear and learning to put a brave face on the world we learn to despise all forms of weakness. We learn systematically to discount any feelings of fear and not to show our feelings to ourselves.

A remark by Sue Cartledge, printed after her death, shows the way women are also deeply affected by this self-repression while also sharing a different vision and hope:

I have always clung to a false idea of strength – the

suppress it all, stiff-upper-lip model. But real strength is recognizing your own weakness and allowing others to see it too.

I must free myself from the tyranny of the past before it destroys any more of the present and the future.

I so desperately want somebody else to be my solution. But I should know by now that it's an impossible dream. Of course another person can seem to bring great happiness for a while. But unless you can resolve your own problems, they will sink it in the end. And the great happiness you feel comes from *you* – from your own capacity for love and joy which romance (temporarily) liberates.[7]

It can be hard for men to accept that 'real strength is recognizing your own weakness', since this threatens our very sense of masculinity. By estranging ourselves from our feelings we block whatever access we might otherwise develop to our inner lives. We learn to respond almost automatically to others, by behaving in the way that is expected of us rather than by responding to an inner sense of ourselves. Often this means doing things for others when we don't really want to. If this seems to contrast with a feminist criticism of men's learned selfishness and thoughtlessness, at another level it helps explain it. Responding automatically produces its own form of personal insensitivity and blindness, though men can largely remain unaware of this within a moral tradition that tends to identify moral behaviour with acting from an autonomous sense of duty.[8]

Men find it hard to acknowledge that 'strength' is a false idea. We fight any such recognition since it compromises our very sense of masculinity. The dominant traditions of social theory maintain a silence over these issues; they are safely relegated to the 'private sphere'. Serious consideration of people's relationships to themselves, an important theme in Marx's early conception of alienation, is blocked by the marxist language of social relationships, which tends to treat these considerations as aspects of 'bourgeois individualism'.[9]

Not only does such language make us insensitive to ourselves, it blinds us to the hurt we do to others in our relationships. We can use our power in relationships to encourage others to deny their own feelings of vulnerability and weakness. We do not want to be reminded of the hurt and pain we carry ourselves; this can make it difficult for women and other men to show their pain to us. If they do so, we may treat this as an occasion to show our own strength as we offer shoulders for support, whilst we do not recognize the distance that is being created in the relationship. In this way we can keep our vulnerability in check.[10]

Though it is strange to acknowledge it, as men we grow up without ever really learning to care for others. We expect women to care for us but we don't really know *how* to care for them. We are so concerned with defending our own position in the world of work and with sustaining our sense of individual achievement, that we desperately want our partners to identify themselves with our success. Women have traditionally been brought up to make this very identification. They have learnt to put the interests of others before their own; they have thereby learnt automatically to discount their own individual needs and wants. This means they have learnt to expect little emotional support from men. Women are beginning to recognize how little they get in their emotional relationships with men. I've been constantly challenged for not giving enough of myself in my relationships, though it has taken time to grasp what this means.

Caught up in the competitive world of work, men can experience any demand from their partners as a kind of betrayal. Often men feel – or at least, they tell themselves – that they are working, not for themselves, but for their wives and children. Such men experience themselves as living at the edge of frustration; they therefore expect to be esteemed, not challenged, in intimate relationships. They feel the support of partners is owed to them so that they can successfully compete against other men. This is what makes men react so impulsively and aggressively when they are told that they aren't giving enough in their relationships. As men, we expect our partners to do the emotional work in supporting us at work, but we resent it if demands are made on us to respond more openly in our emotional relationships. Sometimes it is easier to participate more actively in domestic work and child care than it is to change the tone and character of our emotional and sexual relationships. Often we simply don't understand what is being asked of us. We dismiss the demand as emotional and silently hope that it will go away.

In my own experience in the difficult days of early fatherhood I immediately felt defensive or called upon to say things were going better than they were, rather than simply acknowledging how difficult it was for a new mother in the early months of a new baby. I know how I resisted learning this, thinking that somehow I was being blamed, that if only I had been willing to do more, things would have been better. I couldn't realize that it was an acknowledgement that was wanted and that I was only making things worse and being false to myself in attempting to put a good face on things.

It's the idea of it always being a question of *doing* more that is so tied to the masculine self. Men often think we should be able to cope with any situation that life presents us with. The more our sense of male identity is tied up with work and the protestant ethic the more we are constantly pushing ourselves beyond our limits, thinking that we thereby make ourselves invulnerable to the criticisms of others. In this sense our masculinity has attempted the superhuman; we are left with little sense of our individual limits. We exhaust ourselves taking on much more than we can manage, proving our very sense of masculinity in constantly pushing ourselves against our limits. We barely acknowledge our own tiredness. If employed, we work as if we are machines oblivious of our own bodily needs and remain strangely proud of doing this ourselves. Often we so exhaust ourselves at work that we have little left for our emotional and sexual relationships. We are drained and empty. We are oblivious to the economy of our energies. But because we are so exhausted it is difficult to listen to demands when we get home. The truth is we may have wasted ourselves at work. We remain creatures of the protestant work ethic in our lives, even though we may have broken with it intellectually. It is written into our very conceptions of socialist politics and practice, so that we usually end up taking it for granted.[11]

Since we can so easily discount our own emotional needs and wants it can be difficult to respond to the needs and wants of others. As we become more sensitive to and of ourselves we can become more open to others. But we cannot decide, simply as an act of will, to be more sensitive and open to our partners. This is difficult for us to admit since as men we are brought up to assume we can do anything we put our minds to. This brings us face to face with an area of personal powerlessness, though we will do anything before acknowledging it. We refuse to admit that our education into masculinity might have left us emotionally undeveloped, without the control of our lives and relationships, which comes from thinking we *can* change through an act of will. This is something that John Stuart Mill had to learn about himself. In his *Autobiography* he talks of the extreme rationality of his upbringing and the way this education had left him crippled emotionally.[12]

We prefer to sustain the pretence of being able to cope with emotional situations that we can barely grasp. We can hide an endemic fear of personal emotions and personal conflict behind a wall of personal disdain. We protect ourselves with our own rationality. We can fail to acknowledge our own deep hurt which we carry from childhood since we can only think of this as weakness. We fear that if we allow our softer feelings to surface we shall never be able to regain control of ourselves. It is this form of wilful ignorance and fear of the personal that has come to characterize contemporary masculinity. It unifies men who would otherwise conceive the world in very different political terms.

A fear of intimacy has held men in terrible isolation and loneliness, though this is rarely acknowledged. Usually men have few close personal relationships; we grow up learning to be self-sufficient and independent, learning to live in a world of acquaintances. We learn to despise our own needs as a sign of weakness and to fear any forms of dependency, especially ones we cannot control. If we ask very little from our partners, we do expect them to do our emotional work for us. But since we are largely unaware of these needs we rarely appreciate others for doing this. This becomes another part of invisible female domestic labour.[13]

Since we have such little sense of our own needs it can be difficult to appreciate the needs of others. This is partly what has made women seem so unintelligible to men. But men have rarely appreciated this as a brutalization of our own natures or had much sense of how traditional notions of masculinity could be a 'tyranny', able to destroy both our present and future relationships. Even our existing theories of ideology fail to do justice to the material significance of our sexual identities, since they tend to treat them as emotional and thereby beneath rational consideration. Where our sexual identities are treated as social and historical contructions we are left with little sense of their inter-relationship with a developing sense of self. This gives us little awareness of the contradictions individuals are left with or of the ways people can change.

We fail to acknowledge, even to ourselves, the importance of others; we fail to let others know how important they are to us. This is connected to a fear of loss and separation. We can think that if we let our partners *know* that we love and need them we are somehow compromising our independence. Usually this is thought about in terms of 'freedom', though it is more often connected to a fear of intimacy and commitment. It is almost second nature to us to withhold ourselves emotionally. We fear our own vulnerability, are scared of what it might reveal about ourselves. Often it is only in the context of sexuality that we can allow ourselves to be close and intimate. This is sometimes the only way of reaching a little closer to ourselves.

Because intimacy is feared, many men turn to pornography, which seems to offer the excitement without the personal vulnerability. This is a way of feeling sexual without having to feel intimate. It becomes easy to confuse our needs for intimacy with our needs for contact and sexuality. Our sexual needs are given more public recognition and seen to confirm our masculinity rather than threaten it. For this reason we go for sexual contact as a way of fulfilling our needs for dependency. Somehow these have been made difficult to identify, let alone acknowledge. Often we end up attempting to fulfil a whole range of separate, even contradictory needs in our sexual contact.

Because we are unused to making crucial differentiations for ourselves we can end up feeling dissatisfied. Since we don't have a language in which to identify our emotional and sexual needs and since the very recognition of needs compromises our masculine control, we seek to satisfy our different needs without really being able to identify them. Our needs remain undifferentiated. We might simply want to be held and nurtured but acknowledging this very passivity seems threatening. We can blame our partners for not being ready to interpret our needs for us without ever realizing the pleasure and tension we have put into our sexual contact. But this is simply to shift a responsibility which is ours.

We can assume that we have to be constantly active in our sexual encounters. This is why we feel fear if women take a more active role in sexual relations. We seek to place strict boundaries upon this activity without really facing up to the issues of equalizing sexual pleasure that are involved. But it is also because sex becomes orgasm orientated within heterosexual relations that we can feel nervous and uneasy if our sexual encounters don't reach orgasm. It is so easy to assume that our sexual contact has little to do with the depth and quality of our personal relationship. We can prefer to see sex as an autonomous sphere which has little to do with closeness and intimacy.

This is to treat sex as a commodity rather than challenge

this bourgeois conception.[14] Unfortunately it is this undifferentiated conception of shared human needs that has so often been made an integral part of historical materialism. The left has reproduced this notion by seeing sex as a 'physical need'. So it becomes impossible to recognize that in clarifying our sexual needs we are also defining our individualities. These are needs which are shaped within the context of developing a relationship with a partner. As we learn to define the type of touch and contact we like we also have to realise that our needs will not always be met. Sex has to be negotiated and this can mean learning to respect the differences in what we want for ourselves.

This means being open to discovering what our indivdual emotional and sexual needs are at the moment, recognizing that they can change later. This also means learning to be vulnerable and learning to risk ourselves with others. As we formulate our desires and needs we are learning to reappropriate significant parts of ourselves. This can mean identifying our needs for dependency and passivity as well as, at different times, our needs to be active and independent. This involves taking individual responsibility for our sexual lives as we learn to voice our needs in a clear and open way. But this is threatening to the control we have grown up to assume as men. We have to be open to discovering our needs for ourselves. This is no longer a matter of using our bodies as instruments to satisfy sexual desire, but learning to respond to the needs of our bodies as they emerge.

This can be a very anxious process; it questions inherited notions of male sexuality which are built upon power as a matter of control – getting others to do what we want is often the core of masculine fantasies about sex. As we deepen the contact we have with our own bodily experience and learn to listen to our bodies we begin to appreciate just how estranged we have been from our emotional lives. We begin to learn the painful costs of the identification of male identity with reason and self-control which depends upon a domination of our emotions, feelings and desires. We can learn to transform our understandings of strength, power and control through these notions coming to have a different meaning and significance as they gradually become rooted in contact with different levels of our experience. Learning to take a different kind of responsibility for our sexual practice and our sexuality is involved in this.

This presents us with a vision of personal change in which our intellects and wills have a part to play within a continuing process in which we are constantly facing ourselves as honestly and openly as we can. I've often felt a deep resistance to articulating and negotiating my sexual needs. I want my partner to be able to respond to me intuitively and I recognize some of the ways that language can so easily get in the way. This expresses a deep masculine fantasy about sexuality. We are often left with a dream that has little to do with the experienced reality of our sexual lives. This connects to the difficulties we may have in recognizing our partners as equal sexual beings rather than as extensions of ourselves. It is as if we inherit the deep cultural myth present in Freud's conception of sexuality, that women are fundamentally there to provide pleasure for us. We feel this, though at another level we share the culture's fear of pleasure and so the fear of sexual pleasure as undeserved. This partly explains why we can feel that we have to take our pleasure in silence.

There is another sense in which we fail to take responsibility for our sexual lives. We grow up to see others as the source of our happiness and pleasure. As Sue Cartledge says in her diary 'I so desperately want somebody else to be my solution.' Sexuality has been turned into a measure of individual achievement and success. Sex becomes an issue of masculine conquest and performance which reflects upon the male ego. Not only does it become difficult to ground our sexuality in the contradictions and tensions of continuing personal relationships but it becomes hard to give sexuality a centrality and importance in our lives. It simply becomes another autonomous area in which we are forced to prove ourselves as men.

The marxist emphasis upon production has marginalized

a serious discussion of sexuality and the sexual relations of power. It fails to deal seriously with what it means to assume responsibility and control in the different areas of our lives. It is nervous of thinking in terms of individual responsibility at all, unless it has to do with the moralism and self-denial that is expected of a person who is to be 'seriously' considered as a revolutionary. But if socialists cannot even take responsibility for our own lives and relationships, what are we offering to others? We have been trapped in a particular rationalist myth which offers us overall control of the larger society through the workings of our reason, but has left us ignorant and unaware of ourselves. This is another version of the familiar idea that work has to come first in the protestant ethic.

Fear, masculinity and sexual identity

When I give attention to the notion of sexual development I find myself thinking of Freud's account of a boy's Oedipal resolution since this was an attempt to theorize an experience that is often hidden. As he says 'In boys . . . the complex is not simply repressed, it is literally smashed to pieces by the shock of threatened castration.' At least Freud helps us recognize fear at the core of our sexual identity as boys and shows us its importance in facing the dynamics and consequences of male sexuality. We are shocked, he argues, into giving up our sexual desires towards our mothers by the threat of castration from our fathers.[15] This shows the level of risk and tension attached to sexual feelings, so we should hardly be surprised if we later have difficulties acknowledging these feelings let alone integrating them into our continuing sense of self. Our sexual feelings are culturally represented as free-floating so that we barely have to take responsibility for them. This inevitably minimizes the risk of our sexual feelings, even if it makes it harder for us to own and integrate our sexual experiences. Within Freud's account we can begin to think how we are left feeling that our sexual feelings towards our mothers are wrong and then that these feelings in general are wrong. We are made aware of the threat of our fathers as rivals and we are forced to repress our sexual feelings even though they are deeply embedded. Fear and repression are at the core of the formulation of masculine sexuality in Freud's account. Nancy Chodorow's *The Reproduction of Mothering* points out how this relationship weighs on boys:

> Compared to a girl's love for her father, a boy's Oedipal love for his mother, because it is an extension of the intense mother–infant unity, is more overwhelming and threatening for his ego and sense of (masculine) independence . . . . This mother-son love threatens her husband and causes him to resent his son. The intensity of the Oedipal mother-son bond (and the father-son rivalry) thus causes its repression in the son.[16]

Freud shows a deep connection between the formation of male sexuality and the fear of castration, and he goes some way to recognizing the sex-negating character of European culture, which despises the body and denies it as a source of pleasure, even though this has been our primary relationship and source of identity. As boys we fear retaliation for our desires; this sharpens our need to repress love for our mothers. We learn to fear our own sexual feelings, lest we are unable to control them, finding it hard not to experience the very existence of sexual feelings as tantamount to the realization of a relationship. It is as if the feelings reveal the reality of a brutish nature. Unfortunately psychoanalysis too often denies Freud's initial insights into sexuality, so itself becomes part of a sex-negating culture rather than subverting it.

This fear is a source of deep ambivalence which can show itself in the guilt some men feel when they become aware of their treatment of women. Often the first challenge of feminism is met by an attempt of men to forsake their very masculinity, as if they feel guilty, not simply for what they have done to women but also for the fact of being men. Perhaps this tendency connects to the primal guilt men feel in relation to the love we share for our mothers. Not only are we forced to forsake these feelings out of fear of revenge and castration but also we have to compromise the integrity of our feelings as we are bought off with the benefits of masculinity into identifying with our father who would have otherwise crushed us.

Freud's theory gives some insight into a possible source of the ambivalent feelings many men feel towards masculinity, and the way this connects to the treatment of our mothers. It helps explain why men distance themselves from the explorations of men's consciousness-raising groups by saying it isn't an issue for them since they have no difficulties relating to women and that, in any case, they feel closer to women than they do to men. If we think of the fear we have as boys for our fathers in the Oedipal story, it is hardly surprising that boys (and men), feel such uneasy feelings towards other boys (and men), though this also has to be placed in the context of competitive relations in the larger society. Our identification with the father is built upon fear and anxiety at this transition in our sexual identity though this is something we bury for ourselves. As Chodorow described the situation:

> A boy gives up his mother in order to avoid punishment, but identifies with the father because he can then gain the benefits of being the one who gives punishment, of being masculine and superior.[17]

This begins to show the extent to which notions of male superiority are tied in with the development of a masculine heterosexual identity. We also find possible clues towards some of the sources of the splits in contemporary masculinity. It can help us think about why we find it hard to bear ambivalence and want to use our reason to decide about situations once and for all. Traditional conceptions of morality become tied to issues of masculinity; we realize that, as men, we are taught to think in terms of principles and in terms of right and wrong. This is the way we seek to organize and control our personal relations. So, for instance, we find it hard to accept the strength of feelings we might have both for and against ending a relationship. We want to think that if the decision was 'right', if we worked things out rationally, then we shouldn't feel all this pain of separation. We shouldn't feel the need to mourn a relationship we have chosen to end. We struggle to make our feelings fit our rational perceptions. Freudian psychoanalysis can often encourage rather than challenge this tendency of thought when it is trapped in its own intellectualizations and language. But this is also deeply embedded in the superiority we grow up to feel towards the emotionality and feelings of women. At one level we protect ourselves from being threatened by women we are close to because we are so assured of our superiority. These feelings of superiority run deep; possibly it is a way of dealing with the primal betrayal of our feelings by our mothers. This is a way we betray core feelings and loyalties in ourselves. We are forced to sacrifice our integrity so that after this it can be difficult to trust our feelings and emotions and a slow process to regain a sense of what we want for ourselves, rather than what we think we ought to do or want. This is a way of dealing with the hatred we would otherwise carry for our fathers.

As Freud recognizes, 'It is only in male children that we find the fateful combination of love for the one parent and simultaneous hatred for the other as a rival.'[18] We learn to control our hatred for our fathers through coming to identify with them, whilst at the same time learning to disown the feelings of love and affection we have for our mothers. But Freud tended to universalize these processes, rather than to illuminate the way they grow out of a particular form of family relations.

The Freudian story can easily tempt us into thinking in its own terms. It makes it difficult to show the historically specific constellation of relationships within which a particular form of masculinity is developed. This isn't simply the context in which relationships develop, but forms the very texture and quality of these relationships themselves. The separation of work and domestic life has created a situation in which a wife is as much in need of a husband as children are of a father. This has encouraged women to turn their attention and interest to the next obvious male – the son. With the undermining of patriarchial power of fathers in the family, through de-skilling of work and changes in the capitalist labour process, fathers could be thought of as, and think of themselves as, dispensible.[19] Though this will have left some men with a sense of freedom to pursue their work, at another level it helps explain the growth of jealousy that Freud mentioned. This could well affect the intrusions and inconsistencies fathers make as authority figures within the family and the tone of resentment they express towards their children. Sometimes women cease to feel sexually interested in their absent husbands as they learn to discover a form of sexual satisfaction in relation to their sons. Chodorow hints at the way fathers are excluded and exclude themselves from family relationships:

> Just as the father is often not enough present to prevent or break up the mother-daughter boundary confusion, he is also not available to prevent either his wife's seductiveness or his son's growing incestuous impulses . . . He projects his own fears and desires on to his mother, whose behaviour he then gives that much more weight.[20]

Though Chodorow's work has been important in opening up this discussion, it often remains trapped within the psychoanalytic categories themselves. She introduces different schools of psychoanalytic thought in a useful way but it is often unclear how we are to decide between them. This is unfortunate since her discussion challenges the formal and universal character of Freud's Oedipal theory. This partly emerges from her focus on object relations but this itself minimizes the significance of sexuality, seeing this as an aspect of an instinct theory found in Freud. This fosters its own intellectualization of sexuality, though it offers more useful starting points for understanding the relationship between psychoanalysis and masculinity than a structuralist theory blinded through its prioritization of language, which is unable to put language in the context of social and personal relationships of power and subordination, since it is assumed to structure and organize these relationships themselves.

But it does help to show the ease with which, as men, we can take our resentments out on those closest to us. It becomes second nature for us to assume a position of superiority towards women, even when we have tried to share domestic work and child care. We take up a judgmental position towards the efforts of others with the implicit notion that we really could have done better ourselves. So it becomes hard to acknowledge fully all the effort and attention that has gone into, say cooking a meal or choosing presents. As men we so much take these activities for granted that when we do them ourselves we turn them into an exhibition of individual skill, or else devalue their significance through squeezing them around the more central activities of our day. We can sense the deep sources of some of this behaviour in the ways our masculine sexual identity is established through feeling superior to women we are close to and through establishing our sense of individual identity in a masculine competitive world. It is as if we only know how to feel good ourselves if we put others down. The depths of male competition seem to resist change, even once men become aware of them. Possibly it is because our identities can be established in these realms. Since boyhood our relationships with women are used as ways of proving our esteem with other boys.

According to Chasseguet-Smirgel all children must free themselves from their mothers' omnipotence in order to achieve a sense of autonomy and independence.[21] As Chodorow describes this process, 'His penis and masculinity both compensate for his early narcissistic wound and symbolize his independence and separateness from his mother.'[22] But this is at the cost of identifying masculinity and independence as having no need for affection or vulnerability. Since our sexual feelings echo a primal loss of the mother and remind us of the guilt we feel at betrayal, both of our own feelings and of our relationship with her, they can be experienced as external happenings which we only with difficulty experience as deeply integrated with our personalities. We come to fear our own pleasure.

I think this helps explain the ease with which men can 'cut-off' from our relationships. We've learnt to compartmentalize our feelings so that we can carefully control them. But this very 'cut-off' quality can hurt our developing sexual relationships and make it difficult for us to learn to take initiative and responsibility in them. It makes our relationships incidental, despite acknowledging their importance verbally; it makes our feelings unclear. Even though we are often not aware of it we insist on controlling the terms of the relationships we are in. We get irritable if things aren't done our way and we resist giving up control. Women often bring up issues in relationships which we find hard to give time and attention to, even though we say we want too. Then we are inevitably surprised at the intensity of the feelings our partners have, but this only shows how out of touch we have been with the relationship as our energies and attention have been elsewhere. It is because women have been brought up to find satisfaction and identity in pleasing others that these tensions are held beneath the surface. Sue Cartledge in the collection *Sex and Love* shows how feminism has clearly exposed this aspect of partriachial morality:

> As women we are brought up to be 'unselfish' and more aware of other people's needs than our own. This is the pattern on which countless women have moulded their lives. However, martydom is not so simple. Suppressed desires have a way of resurfacing as resentment. A woman learns 'to give to others out of the well of her own unmet needs'. But the well starts to boil with fury, runs out in gullies of bitterness, dries up.
>
> 1974: When I came back I started to cry with frustration. Then I shouted at Stefan – all kinds of things

came out. That we always did what *he* wanted, made love or not when *he* wanted; that I didn't have the strength of will to decide what I wanted to do, and do it . . .[23]

I can hear the cry of anger and frustration as if it is directed at me. It is all too familiar, even though I pretend to understand it intellectually, I am always surprised and shocked when this happens. I recognize that something is terribly wrong but I don't really know what to do about it. I'm shaken by the fury and the bitterness. I find it hard to accept that things can be that bad, though I know at some level they are. Part of me just wants to flee or withdraw. It is as if all long-term heterosexual relationships in our time are doomed. For all my efforts at a more equal relationship I have to recognize how blind and insensitive I am. It is harder to know what to do about it.

Often as men we are scared of opening ourselves to a sense of our emotional needs since we have controlled them so tightly for so long. We fear being overwhelmed. We don't want to recognize all the frustrations we put up with in our daily work lives. We want to put a good face on things, even though at some level we know we aren't being honest with ourselves. But honesty and truth have never carried much weight in the capitalist world of work. As women refuse to support us emotionally and demand that we learn to do this work for ourselves, our sense of masculine identity is thrown into crisis. We tell ourselves that we are putting up with everything in our work lives to support wives and children and that we aren't asking for very much in return. This is part of the problem. We are so used to denying our needs that there is little basis upon which we could negotiate a more equal relationship. We so easily feel lost since we have no language in which to articulate these new experiences and fear closer contact with other men at this time of weakness and vulnerability. We assume that others won't really want to know us. We assume that it is only us that is affected.

As this crisis has hit the lives of many men relatively few have sought the support of men's consciousness-raising groups. The need for validation in another relationship with a woman has often been most pressing. The pain of rejection is too difficult to live with. And often there is a deep feeling of bitterness and resentment towards feminism since this is blamed for the break-up of the relationship. Little is learnt.

Feminism and masculinity

Feminism has brought these issues home. It has punctured the pretentiousness of so much rhetoric of the left. It has forced us into taking more responsibility for our relationships, domestic work and child care. This has been one element in the withdrawal from activist politics in the late 1970s. But for many people this has meant a reconsideration of the sources of their political involvement, which has been no bad thing. Socialist men were learning that they could analyse the fate of the international capitalist economy but they were speechless when it came to talking through issues in their sexual relationships. Theoretical traditions on the left seemed incapable of illuminating a crucial area of conflict between women and men. The power men carry in the structure of capitalist society is at a considerable cost in terms of our own emotional capacities, understandings and desires. As men, we had often learnt to put our work first because this was where our identity was formed. We expected our partners to accept this since it was the source of the family's income. This was also the source of our individual power. It was a way in which the demands of women and children could be silenced.

But with the questioning of feminism it became clear that there were areas in our lives where 'the emperor had no clothes'. Men, like myself, got angry, spiteful and jealous as we accused women of being irrational. We did not understand why they were bringing up pain from the past. We didn't want to be faced with our past behaviour, especially when we assumed that this would do no good to anyone and wouldn't be changed anyway; we didn't understand the need for the past to be opened and the pain shared if it was to be purged. We couldn't believe in this as a hopeful sign of redemption since this wasn't a process we were part of. Consciousness raising was still an experience few men had participated in and was often frustrating since it was easier to intellectualize experience than to share it. We could only think that women wanted to hurt and punish us. If we were shocked at the depths of resentment, even hatred, and felt we couldn't recognize ourselves as the figures of total evil, we could only respond defensively.

If we feel hurt and rejected the only solution we know is to find another partner who appreciates us. It is because, at some level, we have never learnt to take responsibility for our emotional lives that we automatically assume that if things go wrong we have been with the wrong partner. The protestant ethic has so damaged our sense of the worthwhileness of our natures, making us incapable of giving joy or happiness to ourselves, that we can only look beyond ourselves for the sources of our contact and nourishment.[24] Even then we can feel this is undeserved. As men we are cast into ceaseless work and activities to prove our worth. Often when we are alone or do nothing we feel lost. It is as if we only exist in the image of others. This is part of the narcissism Freud recognized in the male ego. Men are constantly assertive in the public realm; we seem to have a secure and independent sense of ourselves. But this sense of strength can rarely have deep personal roots in the self, as it is based on quite brittle foundations. Some feminists have overestimated the nature of masculine strength, power and identity. They have presented it too clearly even though they have experienced its contradictions. They haven't understood how uncertain men often are behind their self-assured rationality when they can no longer insist upon the terms of the relationship. This isn't to minimize the strength that is confirmed in our public activities, though this is always a basis for a clear and well-defined sense of individual identity.

A different strength grows out of the capacity to identify our own needs. This involves learning to identify our individual problems and taking responsibility for them, rather than blaming others for them, unless they are actually to blame. We no longer see others as the source of *our* own feelings and emotions, expecting them to make us feel better. There is a traditional vision of relationships in which both partners are seen as incomplete in themselves; they come together to find a new completeness. This means seeking in others what we have never learned to give ourselves. This can have deep sources in childhood if as boys we are looked after by mothers who never give us the space to find ways of nourishing ourselves but are always anxious to do things for us. Then we never learn to take a very basic responsibility for ourselves. This has to do with cooking and cleaning, but it also has to do with learning to identify and fulfil – as opposed to dominating and suppressing – our own emotional needs. This helps produce an expectation of women as people who take the emotional initiative in relationships, this can create its own emotional contra- dictions. We want to have our needs met without having to articulate them since the very acknowledgement of our needs compromises our image of self-sufficiency.

We are fearful that if we ever contact our unmet needs they would be so overwhelming that no one would want to have a relationship with us. We interpret this as weakness. This makes it difficult for us to realize that it is just this kind of sharing that others are demanding of us. It is this which promises to give relationships greater depth. It is also difficult for our partners when we swing between denying that we have emotional needs at all to feeling totally overwhelmed by our needs. But this draws attention to our own disconnection with that type of experience. Taking more responsibility for ourselves promises to create a different sense of balance in a relationship. As Sue Cartledge says, 'the great happiness you feel comes from *you* – from your own capacity for love and joy which the romance (temporarily) liberates.'

As men we have to learn to meet more of our own needs, to give time and attention to ourselves and not dismiss this as 'self-indulgent'. We have to learn to rework the traditional moral distinctions of egoism and altruism that have so often made socialist morality a matter of duty and self-denial. We do not know *how* to give our relationships the priority we say they have for us. This involves learning to live in the present reality of our relationships rather than putting everything off to a future that never comes. To do so involves a radical break with ideas of progress as one aspect of the Hegelian inheritance of marxism that structuralism usefully challenges. It involves exploring what matters to us individually while refusing to dismiss this as individualism, as well as challenging notions of masculine success and ambition, thereby transforming our inherited conceptions of masculinity.

We are no less men because we have learnt to identify our need to be touched and held. Freud realised that sexuality is also a site for regression where many of our infant needs can find expression. But it is only in the context of a close and trusting sexual relationship that we can share our fears, joys and resentments rather than simply hold them in check because we deem them inappropriate or unmanly; only then can we learn to integrate them as parts of ourselves. We have to be open to making discoveries about ourselves and to suspend our judgements of what is 'normal' or 'appropriate'.

Reason, fear and politics

In blocking our fear we block our vulnerability and this has an important impact upon our sexual experience. Freud helps to illuminate some of the sources of this, though he refuses to question the implications this has for the politics of the family. But Freud goes some way towards challenging liberal moral assumptions and explaining why it has been so hard for men to learn to take greater responsibility for our emotional and sexual lives, thinking that our pleasure has always to come from outside ourselves. Unless we learn to develop more of a relationship with ourselves and so learn to give pleasure and satisfaction to ourselves we can never learn to care for and nourish others. This involves facing aspects of our personal histories and feelings that we have denied and repressed, and being ready to work more directly with our emotional and bodily experiences. This is a different vision of personal change which challenges the pervasive masculine assumption that we can change through an act of will. This isn't to deny the idea that men don't change because we largely benefit from the way things are at present. But at a deeper level, Freudian notions of sexuality remain patriarchial and make it impossible to create equal relationships in which the importance of sexual pleasure for each partner is fully recognized. Often we are trapped into a masculine narcissism that leaves us isolated, seeing others as objects of our being and a reflection of our own glory. This is an empty future, though one which bourgeois society never fails to support.

As men we inherit impoverished visions of personal change. We inherit a deep split between the public world of masculine identity and the private world of family and relationships, almost existing as different people within these different spheres, with no sense of how to bring them together. This is no less true of socialist men. We often seek to organize our personal relationships according to the rational criteria of objectivity and impartiality which we know in the public world. This unwittingly becomes reason used as a means to assert our power in relation to women, children and other men. We literally do not know how to think about our personal and sexual relationships in different terms, nor do we realize how coercive we can be.

Neither do we acknowledge this as an impoverishment of a masculine experience which has been so closely identified with rationality. We lose patience when others challenge this version of reality showing us aspects of the situation we ignore. We don't take kindly to the suggestion that we have developed our intellect at the expense of our emotional, sensual and instinctual capacities. We do our best to ridicule these claims. We rarely develop a critique of the form of social relationships which have left us with such a narrow and distorted image of ourselves. But we tend to see the issue in liberal terms, failing to appreciate that what is at stake is not simply the value we put on different aspects of our experience but the *damage* actually done to our capacity to relate to others in free and equal ways. We tend to trap ourselves in a liberal vision in which we think of equality as an attitude of equal respect, making it hard to fully understand the hidden injuries of relationships of power and subordination. It has been important for feminism to challenge both liberal and socialist conceptions of equality and show that we treat others as equals, not simply through taking up an attitude of respect towards them, but through *validating* their experience as much as their ideas, their emotions as much as their beliefs. In the context of developing more equal relationships this has involved a critique of inherited concepts of masculinity and a recognition of how traditional notions of socialism have assumed masculinity to be socially and historically unproblematic.

If Marx's insights into the distinctions between intellectual and manual labour can help us think about the different value given to men's and women's labour in society, they can also serve to reinforce the distinction between public and private that feminism has brought into question. There is no space left for the recognition of the emotional work which women often do, which as Jean Baker Miller usefully shows, is an integral, if invisible, part of heterosexual relationships. This is part of the rationalism in which Marx is often trapped. It is as if he accepts that personal and sexual relationships grow naturally out of the feelings people have for each other so that we can depend upon them to look after themselves. It is only the public world that can be made a world of reason. Often this is why men remain oblivious as crises are developing in our relationships.

But as our vision of individual capacities, emotions and feelings is narrowed so is our critique of social relations. We lose any grasp of the injuries inflicted on people through the social relations of power and subordination. Within a structuralist framework in which individuals are somehow seen as 'constituted' through language and discourse, this can no longer be explored, and we are left preferring one mode of production to another for purely pragmatic reasons. There is no place for morality, even for judgement. Within discourse theory we are left incapable of judging, for instance the brutality and cruelty of fascism, only able to point to the success of fascist ideology in articulating a discourse which brings together a ruling coalition. But as we are left with a marxist theory that is no longer grounded in the experience of the suffering and oppression of working people, since experience itself has been made a suspect notion, we can hardly be surprised at the political shifts to the right of those who most loudly proclaim this reading of Marx. But the issues go deeply into the contradictions and tensions of Marx's own writings. We are not simply looking for a different reading of Marx; rather we find different theoretical traditions uniting in their fear of the personal.

Within rationalist social theory it becomes difficult to acknowledge the place of fear and intimacy in people's lives. As long as we learn to discount our feelings of fear and vulnerability it becomes difficult to realize the place of fear and violence as a means of social control in this society. Adorno recognized that in modern capitalist society violence and the threat of bodily violence had become characteristic means of social control.[25] It has taken feminist theory to show that women have constantly been afraid on the streets without ever allowing themselves to identify and acknowledge a fear constantly with them. People suffer from feelings they can be barely aware of at a conscious level, let alone articulate through language. Often, as men, we use language to keep our feelings in check. We aren't happy with the uncomfortable realities of life, nor do we take kindly to being reminded by our partners of how short we fall of the images we have of ourselves. This is another reason why we prefer theories which make the reality of our experience unreachable so that we can live safely and unchallenged in the myths we create for ourselves. Structuralist attempts to present language as relatively autonomous, rather than placing it within the material relationships of power and subordination, often end up as another form of liberal relativism.

As men we are used to showing ourselves to be capable and in control in our public lives. Our partners know different. But we are so used to discounting our personal experience that we can find it difficult, if not impossible to share more of ourselves. In truth we do not have contact with ourselves nor do we know how to work to create it. It is hard to admit we need the help of others, especially since we are so used to using our reason as a weapon to assert that we are all right and need nothing from others. What is more, the dominant structural traditions of thought within marxism make it impossible to connect our individual experience and developing sense of self with the social and historical structures of the larger society. But we also have to challenge the intellectualist traditions of psychoanalysis which have sought to appropriate a discussion of emotions, feelings and desires as part of an 'inner life' that can be studied completely in its own terms, or else reduced to being a reflection of an external reality. This makes it impossible to theorize the 'inner' and 'outer' as parts of a single experience which is able to grant some kind of independent existence to our emotional and psychic lives. Rather we cannot disconnect it from the tensions and contradictions in the personal and social relationships of power and subordination within which we live our lives.

Men have been involved in a process of change for over a decade in response to the challenges of feminism but, in truth, little has changed. If anything there has been a vehement backlash against feminism and the demands for more equal relationships with men. Relationships seem to be changing for a younger generation, though this is difficult to assess. Consciousness raising has often been difficult and uncomfortable for those men who find it easy to intellectualize experience. A movement concerned to redefine our inherited conceptions of masculinity as we learn to relate differently still seems crucial, especially in a period in which mass unemployment is undermining traditional connections between work and masculine identity. An exploration of the formation of masculinity of children, partly through psychoanalysis, can deepen an analysis that has often remained stuck at the level of role theory.

Therapy, in both its theory and practice, can have an important part to play in bringing us as men into closer contact with our emotional selves and in helping us face, between ourselves, the difficult feelings of rage, frustration and disgust we so often feel for the women who challenge the power we have traditionally taken for granted. Otherwise we can easily take these feelings out on our partners, since as men we aren't used to showing our feelings to other men. But this therapy has to connect to a collective practice that challenges institutional power and definitions of masculinity.

However, if this isn't simply to learn tact and language in our relationships with women, it has to involve a process of learning to take more responsibility for ourselves. I've tried to show that this is no easy task since it involves a challenge to our inherited sense of self, our dominant intellectual and moral traditions, and the ways in which we organize our daily lives. It will also mean facing the rage and resentments we often feel for women, though we are careful, sometimes, not to express this. These are feelings we will have to learn to deal with in our relationships with other men. This will bring us closer to our fear, including homophobia and the fear of showing our weakness and vulnerability to other men. This is part of the process of redefining masculinity. But it makes an enormous difference to know that we are not alone.

Notes and References

1. Introduction

1. Shere Hite, *The Hite Report on Male Sexuality*, London: MacDonald, 1981.
2. Helen Gurden & Jill Hardman, 'Men's Studies' Coventry WEA Course', *Achilles Heel*, Nos 6 & 7, London, 1983.
3. 'Boys Against Sexism', *Achilles Heel*, Nos 6 & 7, London, 1983.
4. Ethel Person, 'Sexuality as the Mainstay of Identity: Psychoanalytic Perspectives', *Signs*, Summer 1980.
5. Louise Eichenbaum & Susie Orbach, *What Do Women Want?*, London: Michael Joseph, 1983.
6. D. Dinnerstein, *The Rocking of the Cradle and the Ruling of the World*, London: Souvenir Press, 1978; N. Chodorow, *The Reproduction of Mothering*, Berkeley: University of California Press, 1978; L. Eichenbaum and S. Orbach, op. cit.; Robert Stoller, *Sex and Gender: on the Development of Masculinity and Feminity*, New York: Pason Aronson, 1968.
7. ACTT 1984 Annual Conference as reported in the journal, *Film and Television Technician*.
8. See Jeff Hearn's account of this in *Birth and Afterbirth: A Materialist Account*, London: Achilles Heel Publication, 1983.
9. Kestrel's series for Channel 4, 'About Men' – first shown on British TV in September 1983.

2. Roots of masculinity

1. Dr Gunter Dönner, Director of the Institute for Experimental Endocrinology at Humboldt University, East Berlin, is a leading proponent of the 'nature' argument. For him male and female sexual characteristics, including sexual identity and behaviour, are determined prior to birth. Essential to his theory are the sexual hormones which play the primary role in determining the

differentiation of the sexes. Through their organizational effect, these hormones ultimately influence the hypothalamus, producing either a male or female brain, which in turn determines either male or female behaviour. (See Durden-Smith and de Simone, 'Birth of your Sexual Identity', *Service Digest* 1983, Vol. 9 pp 86–8.)

In contrast to this biologically determinist approach, the theories of John Money at John Hopkins University offer an interactional view in which biological and social/biographical factors participate together in the process of gender formation. According to Dr Money, each stage of foetal development from fertilization to birth is part of a progressive sequence of development, where each programme of a previous stage directly influences the next stage of differentiation. Once a particular programme completes its course it has no further effect on later stages of the development of gender identity. (See John Money and Abe A. Ehrhardt, *Man and Woman, Boy and Girl*, Baltimore: John Hopkins University Press, 1972.) For Money, biology plays a significant role in the formation of gender, specifically in the differentiation of male/female morphology. In the end, however, social/biographical factors predominate in the total process, and – this is crucial to his theory – they can override the genetic or biological sex of an individual. Through social transmission, the process of gender formation begins at birth, from the moment the infant is assigned its sex when the parents see its genitals. The parents and others responsible for the rearing of the child will continue to reconfirm that the child is either male or female through their daily interactions with him or her. Money further claims that hermaphrodites and individuals with discrepancies between internal and external sexual organs will remain secure in their assigned sex if their parents are unambiguous about the sex of their child.

More recently, Money's theories received a serious critical blow when his claims about a theoretically important case were discredited. A male identical twin, because of a medical accident which involved the loss of his penis, was surgically altered at birth and raised as a girl. This case, according to Money and others, clearly exemplified the strength of learning over biological determination. However, during the research for a television documentary, it was discovered that this now adolescent girl was exhibiting serious adjustment problems with regard to her gender.

In fact, some specialists working with her thought that she might never make the adjustment.

These findings do throw some doubt on Money's claims that learning (social/biographical factors) take precedence over biological factors. However, the evidence is not sufficiently conclusive to totally rule out the influence of learning, as Dönner would have us believe. The biological determinists have yet to demonstrate exactly how biological factors, such as hormones, directly affect discreet bits of behaviour. Until this happens, one has to assume that biology plays a significant but predispositional role in the formation of gender, while psychological factors determine the detailed aspects of one's gender identity.

2. Sigmund Freud, 'The Dissolution of the Oedipus Complex', *Collected Papers, Vol. XIX* London: Hogarth Press, 1929.

3. Robert Stoller; *The Transsexual Experiment*, London: Hogarth Press, 1975.

4. *Ibid*.

5. R.R. Greenson, 'Dis-identifying from the Mother: Its Special Importance for the Boy', *International Journal of Psychoanalysis*, Vol. 49, pp 370–74, 1968.

6. Robert Stoller, *The Transsexual Experiment*, London: Hogarth Press, 1975.

7. *Ibid* p. 294.

3. Male sexuality in the media

Further Reading:

Andrew Britton, *Cary Grant: Comedy and Male Sexuality*, Newcastle-upon-Tyne: Tyneside Cinema, 1983.

Susan Brownmiller, *Against Our Will*, London: Penguin, 1977.

Tony Eardley, 'Masculinity Acquitted', *Achilles Heel*, No. 5, London, 1982.

Nancy M. Henley, *Body Politics: Power, Sex and Non-verbal Communication*, Hemel Hempstead: Prentice-Hall, 1977.

Paul Hoch, *White Hero, Black Beast*, London: Pluto Press, 1979.

Wendy Holloway, '"I just wanted to kill a woman". Why? The Ripper and male sexuality', *Feminist Review*, Issue 9, pp 33–40.

Marion Jordan, 'Carry On . . . Follow That Stereotype' in J. Curran and V. Porter (Eds), *British Cinema History*, London; Weidenfeld & Nicholson, 1983.

Annette Kuhn, *Women's Pictures*, London: Routledge & Kegan Paul, 1982.

Michael Malone, *Heroes of Eros*, New York: E.P. Dutton, 1979.

Andy Medhurst and Lucy Tuck, 'The Gender Game' in Jim Cook (Ed), *Television Sitcom*, British Film Institute Dossier No. 17, pp 43–55.

Margaret Walters, *The Nude Male*, London: Paddington Press, 1978.

4. Pornography

1. California Department of Justice estimate cited by Henry Schripper in 'Filthy Lucre', *Mother Jones*, Vol. 5, No. 3, USA, April 1980.

2. A number of feminists have explored the relationship between the imagery of soft pornography and advertising as part of a critique of pornography and the position taken by such groups as WAVAW. See, for instance, Rosalind Coward, 'Sexual Violence and Sexuality', *Feminist Review*, Issue 11, Summer 1982; Kathy Myers, 'Towards a Feminist Erotica', *Camerawork*, No. 24, March 1982 and 'Fashion 'n Passion', *Screen*, Vol. 23, No. 3/4, September/October 1982.

3. An exception is the article 'How I gave Up Pornography', by John Rowan in *Achilles Heel*, No. 6/7, 1982.

4. Andrea Dworkin, *Pornography: Men Possessing Women*, London: The Women's Press, Laura Lederer (Ed), 1981. See also *Take Back The Night: Women On Pornography*, New York: William Morrow & Co., Inc., 1982.

5. Shere Hite, *The Hite Report on Male Sexuality*, London: MacDonald, 1981.

6. These trends are based on the analysis provided by the Conference of Socialist Economists' Political Economy of Women Group in 'Women, the State and Reproduction since the 1930s', *On the Political Economy of Women*, CSE Pamphlet No. 2, London 1977.

7. Wendy Holloway, 'Heterosexual Sex: Power and Desire for the Other', in Sue Cartledge and Joanna Ryan (Eds), *Sex and Love*, London: The Women's Press, 1983, p. 137.

8. Tony Eardley, 'Masculinity Acquitted', *Achilles Heel*, No. 5, London, 1981.

9. Stephen Heath, *The Sexual Fix*, London: Macmillan, 1982. p. 69.

10. Maurice Charney, *Sexual Fiction*, Methuen, London: 1981, p. 165.

11. Wendy Holloway, 'Heterosexual Sex' in *Sex and Love*, p. 130.

12. Wendy Holloway *ibid*, p. 132.

13. Cited by Maureen Green, 'Men and Marriage: Time to Let Them In on the Secret', *Woman*, January 14 1984.

14. Angela Carter, *The Sadeian Woman*, London: Virago 1979, p. 16.

15. Angela Carter, *ibid*, pp. 18, 19.

16. Richard Wollheim, 'A Charismatic View of Pornography', *New York Review of Books,* Vol. 27, February 7, 1980.

17. John Berger, *Ways of Seeing*, London: Penguin, 1972.

18. Richard Dyer, 'Don't Look Now – The Male Pin-Up', *Screen*, Vol. 23, No. 3/4, p. 71, Sept/Oct 1982.

19. Barbara Ehrenreich, *The Hearts of Men: American Dreams and the Flight from Commitment*, London: Pluto Press, 1983. See chapter four.

20. Beverly Brown, 'A Feminist Interest in Pornography – Some Modest Proposals', *m/f*, No. 5/6 1981.

21. Deirdre English, 'The Politics of Porn', *Mother Jones*, Vol. 5, No. 3, p. 43, April 1980.

5. Gay machismo

I would like to thank Ronald Grant, Noël Greig, Tom Swan, Pete Freer, Michelle Russell, Andy Metcalf and Paul Crane for their support, advice and criticism.

1. Jane Rule, 'Sexual Infancy', *The Body Politic*, No. 85, July/August, p. 28, Canada, 1982.

2. Ken Popert, 'Race, Moustaches and Sexual Prejudice', *The Body Politic*, No. 94, June, p. 34, Canada, 1983.

3. See Aubrey Walter (Ed), *Come Together*, London: Gay Men's Press, 1980.

4. David Fernbach, *The Spiral Path*, London: Gay Men's Press, 1981, p. 101–5.

5. Michael Silverstein, 'The History of a Short Unsuccessful Academic Career', in Joseph H. Pleck & Jack Sawys (Eds), *Men and Masculinity*, New York: Prentice Hall, 1974, p. 108.

6. Vitto Russo, *The Celluloid Closet*, New York: Harper and Row, 1981, p. 200.

7. Dennis Altman, *The Homosexualization of America*, Boston: Beacon Press, 1983, p. 4.

8. John Marshall, 'Pansies, Perverts and Macho Men: Changing Conceptions of Male Homosexuality', in Kenneth Plummer (Ed), *The Making of the Modern Homosexual*, London: Hutchinson 1981, p. 136.

9. See: Homer Dickens, *What A Drag*, Australia: Angus & Robertson, 1982. Vitto Russo, *The Celluloid Closet*, New York: Harper & Row, 1981. Richard Dyer (Ed), *Gays and Film*, London: British Film Institute, 1977. Parker Tyler, *Screening the Sexes*, New York: Holt, Rinehart & Winston, 1972.

10. David Fernbach, *The Spiral Path*, London: Gay Men's Press, 1981 p. 82–3. For a critique of this book, see Tim Carrigan, 'Of Marx and Men', *Gay Information*, No. 11, Spring, pp. 18–32, Australia, 1982.

11. Felice Picano interviewing Clark Henley, author of *The Butch Manual,* in Christopher Street, Issue 68, Vol. 6, No. 8, USA, 1982.

12. John Rechy, *The Sexual Outlaw*, New York: Dell Publishing Co., Inc., 1977.

6. Violence and sexuality

1. Rosalind Coward, 'Pornography: Two Opposing Feminist Viewpoints', *Spare Rib*, Issue 119, June 1982.

2. Jan Pahl, 'Patterns of money management within marriage', *Journal of Social Policy*, Vol. 9, Part 3, 1980.

3. Susan Brownmiller, *Against our Will: Men, Women and Rape*, London: Penguin, 1977.

4. Peggy Reeves Sanday, 'The Sociocultural Context of Rape – A Cross-Cultural Study', *Journal of Social Issues*, Vol. 37, no. 4, 1980.

5. Julia & Herman Schwendinger, 'Rape, Sexual Inequality and Levels of Violence', *Crime and Social Justice*, No. 16, 1981.

6. See for example Deirdre English, 'The Politics of Porn: Can Feminists Walk the Line?', *Mother Jones*, Vol. 5, No. 3, April 1980, and Paula Webster, 'Pornography and Pleasure', *Heresies*, Vol. 3, No. 4, Issue 12, 1981.

7. See for example Nancy Friday, *Men in love: Men's Sexual Fantasies*, London: Arrow Books, 1980.

8. Andrea Dworkin, *Pornography: Men Possessing Women*, London: The Women's Press, 1981.

9. Vic Seidler, 'Raging Bull', *Achilles Heel*, No. 5, p. 8, 1980.

10. Elizabeth Wilson, *What is to be Done about Violence Against Women?*, London: Penguin, 1983, pp. 19–23.

11. Barbara Ehrenreich, *The Hearts of Men: American Dreams and the Flight from Commitment*', London: Pluto Press, 1983.

12. George Gilder, *Sexual Suicide*, New York: Quadrangle, 1973, p. 23.

13. George Gilder, *Naked Nomads*, New York: Times Books, 1974, p. 10.

14. Konrad Lorenz, *On Aggression*, New York: Bantam, 1969.

15. Elizabeth Wilson, *Violence against Women*, p. 27.

16. *Socialist Worker*.

17. Andrew Tolson, *The Limits of Masculinity*, London: Tavistock, 1977.

18. Vic Seidler, 'Raging Bull' in *Achilles Heel*, p. 9.

19. Julian Wood, 'Boys will be Boys', *New Socialist*, No. 5, May/June 1982.

20. Michele Barrett, *Women's Oppression Today: Problems in Marxist Feminist Analysis*, London: Verso 1980, pp. 63–4.

21. A.C. Kinsey et al., *Sexual Behaviour in the Human Male*, W.B. Saunders, 1948 and *Sexual Behaviour in the Human Female*, Philadelphia: W.B. Saunders, 1953. Shere Hite, *The Hite Report*, and *The Hite Report on Male Sexuality* London: MacDonald, 1981.

22. Shere Hite, *The Hite Report*, pp. 378–81.

23. Andy Metcalf and Paul Morrison, 'Motorway Conversations: Sex in Long-Term Relationships', *Achilles Heel*, No. 6, p. 20, 1982.

24. Angela Carter, *The Sadeian Woman*, London: Virago, 1979, p. 9.

25. Michele Barrett, *Women's Oppression Today*, pp. 58–61.

26. Nancy Chodorow, *The Reproduction of Mothering*, Berkeley: University of California Press, 1979.

27. Peter Bradbury, 'Sexuality and Male Violence', *Achilles Heel*, No. 5, p. 23, 1981.

28. Wendy Holloway, 'Heterosexual Sex: Power and the Desire for the Other' in Sue Cartledge and Joanna Ryan (Eds) *Sex and Love*, London: The Women's Press, 1983, pp. 124–40.

29. Amanda Spake, 'The End of the Road: Analysing a Sex Crime', *Mother Jones*, Vol. 5, No. 3, April 1980.

30. R. Emerson Dobash and Russell Dobash *Violence Against Wives*, London: Open Books 1980.

31. A. Nicholas Groth, and H. Jean Birnbaum, *Men Who Rape: The Psychology of the Offender*, New York: Plenum Press, 1979.

32. Emerge Inc. *Organising and Implementing Services for Men who Batter*, unpublished.

7. Men's sexuality at work

I am grateful to Wendy Parkin, Martin Humphries, Jay Hearn, David Lloyd-Hughes, Alan Goeter, Julia Graham, Gibson Purrell, Andy Metcalf and Jan Davis for discussions and comments on the issues raised in this chapter; and to Sue Moody for typing the drafts.

1. Quoted in David Jenkins, *Job Power: Blue and White Collar Democracy*, London: Heinemann, 1974, p. 40.
2. Karl Marx, 'Economic and Philosophical Manuscripts' in *Early Writings*, Harmondsworth: Penguin, 1975, p. 326.
3. See also Gareth Parry, 'Equal Rights on the Wedding Night', the *Guardian*, 26 July 1983.
4. Robert Quinn, 'Coping with Cupid: the Formation, Impact and Management of Romantic Relationships in Organizations', *Administrative Science Quarterly*, Vol. 22, pp. 30–45, 1977.
5. *Ibid*.
6. Rachel Nelson, *Success Without Tears*, London: Star, 1980, p. 131.
7. Quoted in Quinn, *op. cit.*
8. Reported in Maureen Green, *Marriage*, London: Fontana, 1984, p. 261; also see Rosalind Miles, *Danger! Men at Work*, London: Futura, 1983, p. 320.
9. Harry Johnston, *Executive Life Styles: A Life Extension Report on Alcohol, Sex and Health*, New York: Crowell, 1974, quoted in David Bradford, Alice Sargent and Melinda Sprague, 'The Executive Man and Woman: the Issue of Sexuality' in F. Gordon and M. Strober (Eds) *Bringing Women into Management*, New York: McGraw-Hill, 1975.
10. Bradford, Sargent and Sprague, 'The Executive Man and Woman' in *Bringing Women into Management*, p. 55.
11. Sharon Mayes, 'Women in positions of authority', *Signs*, Vol. 4, pp. 556–68, 1979.
12. Quoted in Rosalind Loring and Theodora Wells, *Breakthrough: Women into Management*, New York: Van Nostrand Reinhold, 1973, p. 113.
13. Lucy Bland, Charlotte Brundson, Dorothy Hobson, Janice

Winship, 'Women "Inside and Outside" the Relations of Production', in Women's Studies Group, Centre of Contemporary Cultural Studies, *Women Take Issue*, London: Hutchinson, 1978, p. 66.

14. R. Miles, *Danger!*, p. 199.

15. Anthony Burton, *A Programmed Guide To Office Warfare*, London: Panther, 1971, p. 67.

16. Cynthia Cockburn, *Brothers. Male Dominance and Technological Change*, London: Pluto Press, 1983, p. 134.

17. Sue Read, *Sexual Harassment At Work*, Feltham: Hamlyn, 1982, p. 21.

18. Jane McIntosh, 'Sexual harassment: you tell us it's *not* a joke', *Cosmopolitan*, October 1982.

19. NALGO, Liverpool, Equal Opportunities Working Party, *Report on Sexual Harassment*, Liverpool: NALGO, 1982.

20. Alfred Marks Bureau, *Sex in the Office: An Investigation into the Incidence of Sexual Harassment*, London: Alfred Marks Bureau, 1982; also see Michael Robinson, 'Are women "whining and wingeing" about nothing?', *The Listener*, 12 August 1982, pp. 7–8.

21. Cary Cooper and Marilyn Davidson, *High Pressure: Working Lives of Women Managers*, Glasgow: Fontana, 1982.

22. Carmel Keely, Hilary Matthews and Carole Leatherwood 'At Last – The Results of the Sexism Questionnaire' *Public Eye* (Camden NALGO Journal), 1983.

23. Leeds TUCRIC, *Sexual Harassment Of Women At Work*, Leeds: TUCRIC, 1983.

24. Anna Pollert, *Girls, Wives, Factory Lives*, London: Macmillan, 1982, p. 142.

25. Sue Webb, 'Gender and Authority in the Workplace', Paper at British Sociological Association Conference, Manchester, April 1982, Mimeo., University of Manchester, p. 22.

26. Karl Marx, *Manuscripts*.

27. Tony Eardley, 'Pin-ups Come down on Building Sites', *Achilles Heel,* No. 4, pp. 28–9, 1980.

28. Elizabeth Wilson, *What Is To Be Done About Violence Against Women?*, Harmondsworth: Penguin, 1983, pp. 13–14. The distinction between non-contact and contact harassment, with the latter taken more seriously, has been reported from discussions conducted with trade unionists for the *About Men* film series for Channel 4. The Leeds TUCRIC report also gives much valuable information on trades union policies and procedures, many of

which tend to be geared more towards dealing with contact forms.
29. The two other incidents have been described in Eardley, 'Pin-ups' in *Achilles Heel*, and Ann Sedley and Melissa Benn, *Sexual Harassment at Work*, London: National Council for Civil Liberties, 1982, pp. 12–13. In the first case men threatened their use; in the second women carried it out.
30. Theo Nichols and Huw Beynon, *Living With Capitalism*, London: Routledge & Kegan Paul, 1977, pp. 25–6.

Further reading

Three texts which contain much useful information on sexuality at work are those by Anna Pollert and Leeds TUCRIC cited above, and Catherine MacKinnon's *The Sexual Harassment of Working Women*, New Haven: Yale, 1979. Three more that are specifically concerned with men are Cynthia Cockburn's *Brothers*, cited above; Michael Korda, *Male Chauvinism: How It Works*, New York: Random House, 1972; and the *Achilles Heel* special issue on men and work cited above. Useful practical texts include the Campaign for Homosexual Equality (CHE) Pamphlet, *What About The Gay Workers?*, London, 1981; Nathalie Hadjifotiou's *Women and Harassment At Work*, London: Pluto Press, 1983; and the TUC's *Sexual Harassment At Work. A TUC Guide and Workplace Programme For Trade Unionists*, London: TUC, 1983. A more theoretical work on the relevance of alienation in sexual politics is Mary O'Brien's book *The Politics of Reproduction*, London: Routledge & Kegan Paul, 1981.

8. Desire and pregnancy

Although pieces of work like this tend to appear under a single name they are rarely a product of one person's efforts. Many thanks to the following for their criticisms, comments and suggestions at various stages of the process: Rosalind Baker, Dermott Killip, Karen Merkel, Andy Metcalf, and Sara Rance.

1. This is the term used by Carol Brown in her essay, 'Mothers, Fathers and Children: from Private to Public Patriarchy', in Lydia Sargent, *Women and Revolution: The Unhappy Marriage of Marxism and Feminism*, London: Pluto Press, 1981.
2. A discussion of the recent history of this development is contained in Joe Interrante's article, 'Dancing Along the

Precipice', *Radical America* 15, 5, 1981.

3. Michael Silverstein, 'The History of a Short, Unsuccessful Academic Career', in Joseph Pleck and Jack Sawyer, *Men and Masculinity*, Hemel Hempstead: Prentice Hall, 1975, p. 45.

4. This form of representation is referred to by Simone de Beauvoir in *The Second Sex*, London: Penguin, 1972, p. 513ff. There is a discussion of it in relation to Renaissance painting, particularly the work of Bellini in the chapter 'Motherhood According to Giovanni Bellini' in Julia Kristeva, *Desire in Language*, Oxford: Blackwell, 1982.

5. Quoted in Ann Oakley, *Women Confined: Towards a Sociology of Childbirth*, Oxford: Martin Robertson, 1980, p. 210.

6. Kathy Myers, 'Towards a Feminist Erotica', in *Camerawork* 24, p. 15, 1982.

7. Michel Foucault, *The History of Sexuality*, London: Penguin, 1981, p. 37.

8. Michel Foucault, *Ibid.* p. 104.

9. Simone de Beauvoir, *The Second Sex*, p. 513.

10. I have confined myself here to literary history. However, there are clear examples in visual art as well – including, for example, the preoccupation Michelangelo had with his relationship with childhood, birth, and his mother. I presume that musicologists will be able to find their own examples.

11. *About Men*, Broadcasting Support Services, 1983. Phyllis Chessler, and Mary Daly, *Gyn(a)ecology*, London: The Women's Press, 1979.

12. This is probably well known to women, and in a different way I have understood it myself. However, my particular usage here derives from that of Rosalind Coward, speaking at a seminar on Romantic Fiction at the ICA in November 1983.

13. The only example of a pornography of pregnancy I have come across is at second hand: that of the magazine *Mom* which is described in Andrea Dworkin's book *Pornography: Men Possessing Women*, London: The Women's Press, 1981, pp. 218–224. She describes this as a 'right-wing' pornography because it emphasizes the phallic triumph of male sexuality. To me the most interesting aspect of her discussion is the relationship between the fantasy which is projected onto and into the women who model for the magazine, and the penetrative symbolism of medical practice – for example, in the caesarian section, which is often used without good reason. A further characteristic of the representation of

pregnancy in pornography, as exemplified by *Mom*, is the connection between pregnancy and bondage which involves a complex psychology of entrapment, violence, and inscription.

14. Roland Barthes, *A Lover's Discourse*, London: Jonathan Cape, 1979, p. 67.

15. Julia Kristeva, *Desire in Language*, p. 238. Kristeva's argument is too subtle and complex to do justice to here. Her central concern is the way in which, through a history of art, desire is constructed and embodied.

9. Fear and intimacy

This is part of a longer work on 'Morality and Desire in Male Sexuality'. I would like to dedicate it to the memory of Sue Cartledge.

I should like to thank all those involved with the Masculinity Research Project at Goldsmith's College, University of London for their help and encouragement.

1. R.D. Laing, *The Divided Self*, London: Penguin, 1961. This book had a particular significance in exploring the whole issue of mental health and politics.

2. Sheila Ernst and Lucy Goodison, *In Our Own Hands: A Book of Self-Help Therapy*, London: The Women's Press, 1981.

3. For a stimulating polemic against this direction of work, which has often silenced people rather than satisfied them, see Stevi Jackson, 'The Desire for Freud' in *Trouble and Strife*, No. 1, Winter 1983. See also Joanna Ryan 'Feminism and Therapy', The Pam Smith Memorial Lecture: Polytechnic of North London, 1983. See also Louise Eichenbaum and Susie Orbach, *Outside In, Inside Out: Women's Psychology, a Feminist Psychoanalytic Approach*, London: Penguin 1982.

4. M. Foucault, *The History of Sexuality*, London: Penguin, 1981.

5. Antonio Gramsci, *The Prison Notebooks*, London: Lawrence and Wishart, 1981. See in particular Part 3: 'The Philosophy of Praxis' pp. 321–77.

6. See Brian Easlea, *Science and Sexual Oppression*, London: Weidenfeld & Nicholson, 1982.

7. *Spare Rib,* May 1981.

8. See Max Horkheimer, *The Eclipse of Reason*, New York: Seabury Press, 1970, and Lawrence Blum, *Friendship, Altruism and*

Morality, London: Routledge & Kegan Paul, 1981.

9. Vic Seidler, 'Trusting Ourselves: Marxism, Human Needs and Sexual Politics' in Simon Clarke et al. (Eds), *One-Dimensional Marxism*, London: Allison and Busby, 1981.

10. See Susan Griffin, *Pornography and Silence*, London: The Women's Press, 1981. Another book of essays that is similarly rich, though barely known in England is Ellen Willis, *Beginning to see the Light*, New York: Alfred A. Knopf, 1981.

11. See David Morgan's essay 'Men, masculinity and the process of sociological enquiry' in Helen Roberts (Ed), *Doing Feminist Research*, London: Routledge and Kegan Paul, 1980.

12. John Stuart Mill, *Autobiography*, Ed. J. Stillinger, Oxford: Clarendon Press, 1971. An attempt to discuss John Stuart Mill within the context of the treatment of women in political thought is made in Susan Miller Okin's *Women In Western Political Thought*, London: Virago, 1981.

13. Jean Baker Miller, *Towards a New Psychology of Women*, London: Penguin, 1978.

14. This is an issue which Eileen Phillips (Ed), *The Left and the Erotic*, London: Lawrence and Wishart, 1983, has helped to illuminate.

15. A useful selection of Freud's writings on the theories of sexuality is to be found in Sigmund Freud, *On Sexuality*, London: Penguin, 1977. For help in situating Reich's assessment of Freud's theory of sexual development see the impressive biography by Myron Sharaf, *Fury On Earth*, New York: St Martin's/Marek, 1983. For the continuing influence of Freud see Wilhelm Reich, *Reich Speaks of Freud*, London: Penguin, 1975.

16. Nancy Chodorow, *The Reproduction of Mothering*, Berkeley: University of California Press, 1978, Chapter 11.

17. Nancy Chodorow, *Ibid*.

18. Nancy Chodorow, *Ibid*, note 15.

19. Max Horkheimer, *Critical Theory*, New York: Herder and Herder, 1972. See also my article on 'Masculinity and Fascism' in *Achilles Heel* No. 1, Summer 1978.

20. Nancy Chodorow, *Reproduction of Mothering*, Chapter 11, note 16.

21. See articles in J. Chasseguet-Smirgel (Ed), *Female Sexuality*, Ann Arbor: University of Michigan Press, 1970.

22. Nancy Chodorow, *Reproduction of Mothering*, note 16.

23. Sue Cartledge, 'Duty and Desire: Creating a Feminist

Morality' in Sue Cartledge & Joanna Ryan (Eds), *Sex and Love*, London: The Women's Press, 1983.

24. The significance of the protestant ethic is usefully described in Erich Fromm's *Fear of Freedom*, London: Routledge & Kegan Paul, 1960.

25. Theodore Adorno, *Minima Moralia*, London: New Left Books, 1978.

A CREATIVE TENSION
EXPLORATIONS IN SOCIALIST FEMINISM
Edited by Anja Meulenbelt, Joyce Outshoorn, Selma Sevenhuijsen and Petra de Vries

Infused with a sense of strategic urgency, these writings by Dutch feminists range over the central areas of debate within the women's movement from an international perspective. They cover the domestic and the public sphere; production and reproduction; motherhood; women's struggle in the Third World; feminism and psychoanalysis; the family.

160 pages
0 86104 756 7   £3.95 paperback

HOLY VIRILITY
THE SOCIAL CONSTRUCTION OF MASCULINITY
EMMANUEL REYNAUD

A controversial essay on the development of patriarchy through history.

128 pages
0 86104 399 5   £3.50 paperback

BROTHERS
MALE DOMINANCE AND TECHNOLOGICAL CHANGE
CYNTHIA COCKBURN

Cynthia Cockburn, researcher and author of the highly acclaimed *The Local State*, reports on four newspaper firms where she talked to fifty skilled craftsmen about their working lives, their union, women as competitors and colleagues, their feelings about class, home life and domestic relationships. The shake-out and restructuring of the workforce could be turned to advantage by trade unions. But she asks: will a genuine working-class consciousness win out over sectional, and sexist, self-interest?

'Cockburn has managed that most difficult of tasks: to produce a book on an important social issue which is theoretically interesting, factually informative and well written.' *New Society*

264 pages. Index
0 86104 384 7 £5.95 paperback

GAYS AND THE LAW
PAUL CRANE

Gays and the Law is a comprehensive account of the law on homosexuality in the UK and how it is used against gay men and lesbians. It shows how the law curtails sexual relationships, living together, work and leisure.

'An important book.' *The Guardian*

256 pages. Index
0 86104 386 3 £4.95 paperback

THE HEARTS OF MEN
AMERICAN DREAMS AND THE FLIGHT FROM COMMITMENT
BARBARA EHRENREICH

Writing with conviction and wit, Barbara
Ehrenreich traces men's rejection of the
breadwinner ethic. She contends that it was
this defiance of 'responsibility', which fuelled
the right-wing, anti-feminist movement.

'Compelling analysis.' *Guardian*
'Written in a lively journalist style, with a
cool undertow of humour . . . a gentle
polemic . . . *The Hearts of Men* is an
admirable piece of feminist strategy.' *City
Limits*
'A good read, and gives an element of hope
to feminists with men in their lives.' *Tribune*

224 pages. Index
0 86104 724 9   £4.95 paperback

GENDER AT WORK

ANN GAME and ROSEMARY PRINGLE

The number of trades and professions in
which women work is increasing.
Newspapers dearly love 'the first woman taxi-
driver' stories. They neglect areas, including
housework, where women's presence is a
long-established reality. The case studies in
Gender at Work — on manufacturing,
banking, the retail trade, computers, nursing
and housework — reflect trends occurring in
all advanced capitalist countries, including
the UK. Its empirical richness makes the book
essential reading for everyone interested in
understanding the link between the
oppression of women through production in
workplaces and consumption at home.

144 pages
0 86104 671 4   £3.95 paperback